Millennium Edition

Deciding What to
Teach and Test

Millennium Edition

Deciding What to Teach and Test

For information:

Corwin Press, Inc.
A Sage Publications Company
2455 Teller Road
Thousand Oaks, California 91320
E-mail: order@corwinpress.com

Sage Publications Ltd.
6 Bonhill Street
London EC2A 4PU
United Kingdom

Sage Publications India Pvt. Ltd.
M-32 Market
Greater Kailash I
New Delhi 110 048 India

Printed in the United States of America

Library of Congress Cataloging-in-Publication Data

English, Fenwick W.
    Deciding what to teach and test: Developing, aligning, and auditing the curriculum / by Fenwick English.—Millennium ed.
        p. cm.
    Includes bibliographical references.
    ISBN 0-8039-6831-0 (cloth: acid-free paper)
    ISBN 0-8039-6832-9 (pbk.: acid-free paper)
    1. Curriculum planning—United States. 2. Educational tests and measurements—United States I. Title.
    LB2806.15 .E54 2000
    375'.001—dc21   99-050510

            03 04 05 06 7 6 5 4

Production Editor:	S. Marlene Head/Denise Santoyo
Editorial Assistant:	Kristen L. Gibson
Typesetter:	Rebecca Evans
Cover Designer:	Michelle Lee

Contents

Foreword

This book is about curriculum in its purest, applied form. In a no-nonsense manner, Fenwick W. English has extracted the very essence of what is known about curriculum and organized it into a highly readable and usable handbook. This book transcends the vague, sugarcoated, pseudoscientific treatments found in much curriculum literature and takes the reader to the heart of curriculum practice, theory, and day-to-day problems in easy-to-understand terms.

Curriculum practice is the heart of this book—the practice and challenges principals and central office curriculum administrators face every day. This book is for school administrators and teachers who want fast, accurate, and easy-to-use answers to the following questions and more:

- How do you develop curriculum?
- Which curricula should be developed?
- How do you know whether the curriculum is being taught?
- What should be tested?
- How do you determine whether it is being taught well?
- Are teaching to the test and curriculum alignment ethical?

- How do you determine whether the written, taught, and tested curricula are one and the same?
- How do you design an efficient and effective curriculum management plan?

Although this book is not a theory book, the content is based on the strongest curriculum theories available. Professor English has interwoven strong curriculum and management theory with proven practice to offer curriculum design and delivery guidelines that the reader can use to ensure maximum student learning. This book represents the "state of the art" in curriculum thinking and practice.

LARRY E. FRASE
San Diego State University

Preface to the Millennium Edition

Americans continue to be fascinated by tests. There are actually several simultaneously different conversations going on about them in education today. Legislators and policymakers fret about test scores as though they were an accurate and solid measure of the educational programs and schools they purport to embrace. The debates about the wisdom of more testing, and even a discussion regarding the claims of what tests do, are seldom heard in the halls of mainstream political discourse at any level in American society. Conversations about them center around cost and content assessed and availability of the results to the media. School test results are now spread over the pages of the press like Saturday football scores.

The second conversation is one that is encountered in this book. This is a conversation about the responsiveness of schools and school systems to testing legislation that is designed to improve schools "by testing excellence" in them. It's a well-worn tactic employed by Horace Mann, the "Father of Public Education." In Mann's classic battle with the Boston schoolmasters, he devised a test in secret, had copies printed, and then would take his horse and buggy to a local school, order the teachers to bring all students to the auditorium, and administer the test. After this scenario he would drive away and later release the test scores with a blast at the ineffectiveness and inefficiency of the schools. He used this method to centralize state educational power. We are using the same method to propose decentralization and privatization today. In this scenario, tests are not diagnostic tools. They have become weapons in a test of wills. Schools whose pupil populations do not do well are assumed to be "poor," when the fact is that many are simply organizations serving the poor.

Most practicing educators know that many tests have little to do with any local, state, or national curricula. Any cursory "eyeball" analysis of such scores in the local media after the test results are released will inevitably show that the highest scores come from the richest areas of the state or city, and the lowest from the poorest areas. The injustices meted out to poor, minority students in the name of tests is a national scandal. They are placed in double jeopardy, first because they are poor, and second because color is related to poverty. What can educators do when tests are used as weapons to punish someone for being poor, black, or Hispanic? The answer is to make sure students are prepared to take the tests. To do this well means to engage in *alignment* and to confront the cult of secrecy that surrounds many testing programs.

If a test is going to serve as a measure of accountability, there can be no secrecy. To be held accountable within the concept of *fairness and due process,* a person must know what is expected, have an opportunity to learn what is expected, and be provided an opportunity to demonstrate whether he or she can actually do the task. Keeping tests secretive violates due process. I've had this conversation with testing bureau personnel of many state departments of education, some of them quite heated. The logic embedded in accountability is not the same logic embedded in tests, particularly the norm-referenced standardized variety. Curiously, in private conversations, most of the representatives of the testing companies who sell the tests on the road agree with me. If they don't, they can't say so publicly. How can the schools do better on tests if they are kept secret? If the tests don't measure any specific curriculum, how can be they used to fairly assess any local or state curricula, the ones most teachers and administrators are really accountable to teach and supervise?

I find the naïveté of some of the testing advocates appalling. When a board of education threatens contractual nonrenewal of a superintendent who somehow can't improve test scores, the idea that one should not "teach to the test" is counterintuitive. The testing advocates want to believe that tests are neutral diagnostic tools designed to "help" schools become better. They ignore 30 years of research that shows that what drives most test scores has nothing to do with what is going on in schools or who is working in them, but is predicated and anchored by the socioeconomic dispositions of school clientele. They want to continue to posture that knowledge is neutral and that the tests are assessing something open and equally accessible and available to all the students who are compelled to take them. They want to continue to believe that all children have an equal start to acquire the cultural capital that is included on test content, including the linguistic skills and conceptual fields in which schools transact their main business. Tests assume that there is a cultural and linguistic homogeneity present which is defied by anyone who is now working in schools which are becoming increasingly more diverse, especially in the nation's urban school centers.

Deciding What to Teach and Test opened this conversation in 1992. It's still going on. I keep working in this vineyard only because of my outrage at the false cloak of impartiality that shields the testing business from the scrutiny it deserves. Tests do not treat all children with equality, let alone equity. The fact that the constant predictors of test performance are grounded in socioeconomic class, race, and gender reveal the deep and biased fault lines which permeate the industry. Many children, as well as the teachers and administrators who work with them, have been and continue to be unfairly labeled and categorized. *Without alignment,* there is nothing fair about testing. *Without alignment,* accountability is a sham. *Without alignment,* there can be no fair judgment about how well schools are really doing.

The rich will continue to perform well, and the poor will continue to be at the bottom of the bell curve. There is no way off the bottom. And if the poor are also black and Hispanic, what does that tell anybody? How will this help the schools? What will become of the children who are stigmatized by tests that have from the beginning categorized them as cultural untouchables?

We are not, as some of our politically conservative critics charge, the children of John Dewey. I wish it were so. We are, rather, the children of Frederick Winslow Taylor. The accountability movement is Taylorism personified, especially in the measurement of work, which testing represents in education. That it becomes fairer is the key to its continuation, though its abolition is probably not possible. At least I should be satisfied with it becoming *fairer.* Many tests in use in education are not now fair, open, or equitable. They remain locked in the false scientism and genetic frauds of the 19th and early 20th centuries that, unfortunately, promise to be extended into the new millennium. That we should initiate the process of untangling this racist, sexist, and class-based system masquerading as meritocracy is long overdue. It begins with alignment. It begins with creating a level playing field. After that, we must begin the process of reexamining the game itself—because alignment still works within the system. The system itself is the problem. Alignment then represents a modest adjustment in an evolutionary process of change.

FENWICK W. ENGLISH
Iowa State University, Ames, Iowa

Preface to the First Edition

This book is about practice and the kind of day-to-day problems principals and central office curriculum administrators, working in schools and school districts, encounter in the area of curriculum, instruction, and evaluation. While it is not a "theory" book about curriculum, it is not devoid of theory. Rather, the theory is embedded in the text itself.

It can be found in the viewpoint expressed about curriculum and its functions in schools, about what curriculum leaders should be doing and thinking, and about how teachers should be working to improve pupil achievement. All of these set up expectations, and it is in response to these expectations that the *theory* behind this book is exposed.

The basic idea behind curriculum in this book is that it is a *means to an end,* and not an end in itself. It is also a political as well as an educational activity. Nobody writes curriculum unless they have to and unless there is some larger purpose in mind. Often, these larger purposes are hidden or not expressed well, particularly the political expressions of curriculum. Practitioners may be unaware of these political realities. They are referenced in this book as the development of *ideologies.* All schools have such ideologies, even by default and even if they aren't aware or conscious of them. Schools are value-laden institutions and espouse certain kinds of values while avoiding or downplaying others. Not to believe this is naive. Curricular and instructional practices are congruent with whatever value system is at work in a school.

The book proposes that there are three forms of curricula in schools: *formal, informal,* and *hidden.* At the same time, there are manifestations of these forms in the *written, taught,* and *tested curricula.* The book shows how these six elements are brought together in working with the development of a localized school or district curriculum.

The function of curriculum is to shape the work of teachers by focusing and connecting it as a kind of *work plan* in schools. It doesn't matter who "develops" it, whether imposed top down or constructed "bottom up," the function of curriculum is to shape the work of classroom teachers.

It does matter who controls curriculum and whether it "controls" teachers and students or whether it helps them become emancipated in our schools. Emancipation would mean that one of the goals of curriculum would be for learners and teachers to come to question the base of authority of the curriculum itself. Few schools now permit such forays. Schools remain places firmly affixed to the larger political system and the dominant powers in them via the expanding state control of education. Testing and technicization of the classroom are devices to expand state and ultimately federal control of curriculum. Already, national goals are being shaped, with a national exam not far away.

The topic of *curriculum alignment* is pursued rather vigorously, particularly as it relates to the "ethics" of testing in schools. At the same time as alignment practices are increasing in the nation's schools, there is a cry from the testing purists that such practices constitute a form of "pollution" of the results. This can only be true if such tests are viewed as assessing a biological as opposed to a cultural set of characteristics. The controversy over what tests assess, and whether the domains of testing are more an expression of genetics or environment, is a long-standing one in education.

The viewpoint expressed in this book is that tests primarily assess cultural differences, which is why socioeconomic level is so dominant as a predictor of pupil performance in most state tests. This is particularly true if tests have a low alignment or "match" to any school's curriculum—the preferred state by test purists. In a situation where a test has a low alignment to a school's curriculum, it cannot be used to accurately measure that curriculum or to make any judgments about the quality of teaching or administrative practices or about the children's learning either. The assessment of children's so-called innate and immutable learning characteristics have little real use in a school, except to engage in labeling students or to develop "tracks" where some students are dumped for their entire school careers in mind-numbing classrooms with diluted curriculum. *Curriculum alignment* may be the lever by which the public and the testing companies have finally come to grips with the hidden assumptions behind mass pupil testing itself. Americans have a penchant for the simple explanation and for *inspection* being a "cure" for most maladies. Educational tests fit neatly into this national proclivity.

The book also deals with evaluation in the form of curriculum auditing. While this topic may strike some as "new," it has been used nationally since 1979 and continues to expand and grow as a practice to assess the system of management of curriculum in schools or school systems. Auditing is a site-based form of evaluation that has the potential to replace accreditation as the accepted form of quality assurance for public education. The chapter ends with a self-assessment that readers can use to determine a school or school system's readiness to undertake a curriculum audit.

The final element is the book's Troubleshooting Guide, which is indexed to the issues and problems highlighted in the book's contents.

FENWICK W. ENGLISH
University of Kentucky

About the Author

Fenwick W. English is a professor and coordinator of the educational administration program in the Department of Educational Leadership and Policy Studies in the College of Education at Iowa State University, Ames, Iowa. He is a former dean of a college of education and vice-chancellor for academic affairs at a regional university in Indiana. He has held professorships at the University of Kentucky, University of Cincinnati, and Lehigh University in Bethlehem, Pennsylvania.

English's practitioner experience in public education includes service as a middle school principal, coordinator and director, assistant superintendent, and superintendent of schools in New York state. He is the author or coauthor of more than 16 books in education. His consulting experience has taken him to 49 of the 50 states and to 9 foreign countries, including Japan and Saudi Arabia. Over the years, he has been a frequent platform speaker at national practitioner conferences including AASA, ASCD, and NASSP, and has presented symposia at UCEA and AERA. He received his BS and MS from the University of Southern California and his PhD from Arizona State University.

1

The Function of Curriculum in Schools

Curriculum design and delivery face one fundamental problem in schools. When the door is shut and nobody else is around, the classroom teacher can select and teach just about any curriculum he or she decides is appropriate. This fact of organizational autonomy represents the shoals of many so-called "reforms" in education: innumerable board policy pronouncements, state testing mandates, national goals, superintendent's decisions, or principal/supervisory dicta.

School structure isolates teachers in self-contained classrooms with children, and alone they can make independent decisions about what they teach. The decisions of a teacher can void the best developed curriculum plans by ignoring them. In fact, as one veteran school principal observed, her school was filled with "B" teachers, that is, they "be" there before her and they "be" there after her. If teachers don't like a curriculum or an unpopular curriculum leader, they can simply wait them out. The permanency of the teaching staff gives them great leverage in "stonewalling" curricular change desired by an impermanent administrative staff.

1.1 What Is Curriculum?

When most administrators think about "curriculum," they think about "curriculum guides." The word *curriculum* didn't come into widespread use in education until textbooks were used in preparing teachers in normal schools. That didn't occur until 1900 (Schubert, 1980). For a very long time, school textbooks took the place of curriculum in the nation's public schools. It was textbooks that established the content to be taught and delineated the methods used to teach them as well. To a very large extent, the domination of the textbook in curricular affairs continues into current times (Perkinson, 1985).

From this historical perspective, it may be seen that *curriculum* is any document or plan that exists in a school or school system that defines the work of teachers, at least to the extent of identifying the content to be taught children and the methods to be used in the process.

Most schools have a variety of such *work plans* in place or available for teachers to use. Such materials may be textbooks, curriculum guides, scope and sequence charts, computer programs, accreditation guidelines, state department of education or state board guidelines, local board policies or their specifications. All of these "plans" compete for the attention and loyalty of the classroom teacher. In many cases, these documents do not "match" one another, may contain contradictory advice or information, or may be so open to interpretation that contradiction arises when they are implemented. *Curriculum* is a *document* of some sort, and its purpose is to *focus* and *connect* the work of classroom teachers in schools (English, 1987). Too often, curriculum is merely a *symbol,* and a hollow one at that, of what the school would like to think its mission or purpose might be. Reality may present a far different picture.

1.2 Curriculum Design and Delivery

Curriculum *design* refers to the act of creating the curriculum in schools. This may involve the purchase of textbooks (one kind of work plan and curriculum) and/or the writing of curriculum guides (another kind of work plan), and neither may be well connected to the other. This presents a real problem in considering the *alignment of curriculum* to the tests in use. School officials like to believe that teachers follow curriculum guides when in fact the research reveals they are much more likely to be dependent upon the textbook as the actual day-to-day work plan or "real" curriculum.

Curriculum *delivery* refers to any act of implementing, supervising, monitoring, or using feedback to improve the curriculum once it has been created and put into place in schools.

1.3 Curriculum Coordination and Articulation

Common in the vocabulary of most curricularists working in schools are the concepts of curriculum coordination and curriculum articulation.

Curriculum coordination refers to the extent of the *focus* and *connectivity* present laterally within a school or a school district. For example, if one were to ask, "What do four teachers of U.S. History I have in common at high school 'X'?" this would pertain to the extent that there was some expected focus and connectivity between these four teachers and their classes in a common curricular area. For *curriculum coordination* to exist, the four teachers do not have to be doing exactly the same thing at exactly the same time. The extent of similarity—that is, focus and connectivity—would be expected to vary some as the teachers adapted the content to be taught to the differences in the learners in their classes.

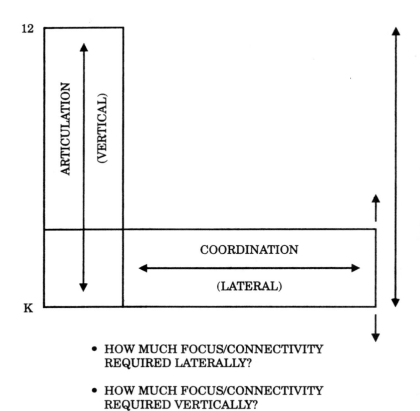

- HOW MUCH FOCUS/CONNECTIVITY
  REQUIRED LATERALLY?

- HOW MUCH FOCUS/CONNECTIVITY
  REQUIRED VERTICALLY?

Figure 1.1. Curriculum Focus/Connectivity Issues

Curriculum articulation refers to the focus and vertical connectivity in a school or school system. For example, if one were
to ask what the level of focus and connectivity were from those
four teachers of U.S. History I to any class of U.S. History II,
one would be questioning the extent of curriculum articulation
present. It would be possible to secure a coordinated curriculum
without necessarily dealing with issues of articulation. One could
have all the teachers in one grade or subject focused and connected without dealing with the teachers at the next grade or
level. The same problem can exist between schools within the
same school district. Figure 1.1 illustrates the commonality and
difference between curriculum coordination and articulation.

TABLE 1.1 Design/Delivery Issues Relating to Curriculum Coordination and Articulation in Schools

Issues	*Coordination*	*Articulation*
Design issues	Define in the work plan the required levels of focus/ connectivity desired to optimize student performance laterally	Define in the work plan the required levels of focus/connectivity desired to optimize student performance vertically
Delivery issues	Monitor program to ensure design integrity laterally	Monitor program to ensure design integrity vertically

1.4 Combining Design/Delivery Issues in Schools

The several dimensions of dealing with curriculum in schools are shown in Table 1.1, which illustrates the possibilities and concerns of design and delivery issues relating to coordination and articulation in schools. On paper, these issues look reasonably simple. In the actual operations of schools and school districts, they become very complex.

Part of the problem in attaining design coordination and articulation is that teachers involved in curriculum construction do not agree on what the desired level of focus and connectivity should be. In part, this concern has been forced upon them by state or local testing programs that resolve these issues by testing students at a given level of focus and specificity. Then, as schools begin to engage in curriculum alignment with tests (a practice called "backloading"), the definition of the test focus and connectivity becomes that of the curriculum.

Of course, teachers are loath to define their work any more precisely than is necessary, because to do so invites a concomitant type of supervision on the part of administrators and supervisors that changes the autonomy they currently enjoy and hence the *control* of their work (see Lortie, 1975). Supervision involves monitoring the fidelity of the delivery of the curriculum compared with its design. This can occur even without interfering with the classroom teachers' usual prerogatives of deciding what kind of methods to use to teach with any given curriculum design.

At the root of this issue is the concept that, once the curriculum content is adequately defined (a design issue), the teacher is obligated to teach it (a delivery issue) in some reasonably competent manner. Supervision involves an estimate of the adherence or fidelity of what is taught (not necessarily how it is taught) to what was supposed to be taught. This is the process of content design to content delivery.

Curriculum articulation is often lost within the structure of schools in which an egg-crate-type physical environment invites and encourages teacher individuality, isolation, and idiosyncratic responses. The issue is accentuated by school building to building autonomy and isolation involving authority within and across school sites.

Many a nice curriculum design, which was designed to enhance focus and connectivity within and across school sites, disappears in the reality of the chasms and gaps in the respective spheres of teacher and administrative autonomy that exist within school districts. This is why school organization has been labeled "loosely coupled" (Weick, 1978).

This organizational "fact of life" is perhaps the greatest barrier to the improvement of test performance, because all testing scenarios implicitly assume that some focus and connectivity are present in the school system, otherwise all commonality would be lost.

The presence of a minimum of commonality is a requirement for a test to provide important information about what is going on in school systems. What tests usually explain is *what isn't going on* in schools and school districts, which is why socioeconomic level remains the biggest predictor of pupil achievement as opposed to the actual curriculum in schools. The minute that curriculum becomes focused on and connected to, as well as aligned with tests, the influence of socioeconomic level on test performance declines. This phenomenon is one of the most important correlates of the "effective schools" movement. These "effective school" procedures, once employed, decrease the predictability of socioeconomic *determinism* from test performance, which means poor kids can do well on tests if they are taught properly and well.

1.5 Different Perspectives of Curriculum in Schools

There are at least three different types of curriculum in schools. One is the *formal curriculum*. That is the one that usually appears in curriculum guides, state regulations, or officially sanctioned scope and sequence charts. This is the one that is debated in public.

The second type of curriculum is the *informal curriculum*. This curriculum represents the unrecognized and unofficial aspects of designing or delivering the curriculum. For example, in *design,* the informal curriculum would represent the "values" at work in selecting curriculum content that is only tangentially "public." Such a value base is always at work when it comes to selecting the content to be included in schools.

The informal curriculum may be the one in *delivery* that is epitomized in various "tracking plans" that group children by ability and then differentiate among them by delivering a very different curriculum. The informal curriculum also involves the subtle but important personality variables of the teacher and the way these interact with students positively or negatively to encourage improved pupil learning.

The informal curriculum also includes learning how to take tests and coming to understand what tests mean to engaging in judgments about students and their potential success in schools. The student becomes increasingly aware that the judgment made about him or her by a teacher represents one that is *total* and often *socially deterministic.* Many come to accept the teacher's definition of their potential as that of society. If the students represent a group at odds with the more dominant group in society that teachers represent, they may come to feel of "less value" as persons (see Bernstein, 1990, p. 171).

Then there is a *hidden curriculum.* This curriculum is the one rarely discussed in schools. It is not even recognized by many educators who work in them. The hidden curriculum is the one that is taught without formal recognition. For example, American children are taught to be "neat and clean," "on time," and "respectful" to teachers. These "lessons" are rarely contained within formal curricula. But they are powerful conventions and norms that are at work in schools nonetheless.

The hidden curriculum contains "structured silences" (Aronowitz & Giroux, 1985) that embody expectations and presuppositions about social conduct that often place disadvantaged students "at risk" in schools and work against them by being ignorant of the inherent cultural biases that are embedded in school rules.

For example, a teacher of Native Americans complained about the lack of respect Indians seem to have for her because they would not look her in the eye. Indians were "shifty," and deceitful in her view, and this was an observable behavior that manifested this trait. This teacher was culturally unaware that, in Indian life, one *does not look directly at* a person respected as being in authority, for to do so would be a sure sign of disrespect. This same characteristic is present in a variety of Asian cultures as well.

Other examples of the hidden curriculum that are distinctly cultural are learning the "correct" speaking distance in relationship to how loudly one talks and how closely one stands to another person in verbal discourse (see Hall, 1977). These "lessons" are all taught in school without being in any "curriculum guide" or textbook.

There are three *other* curricula as well. They are the *written curriculum,* the *taught curriculum,* and the *tested curriculum.* These three curricula deal with content and express the absolute possibility that there could be in schools three unrelated "contents" floating around, unconnected to one another.

Table 1.2 illustrates a 3 × 3 curriculum matrix that contains all six dimensions previously discussed.

Most school administrators only consider the formal written, taught, and tested curricula in their work. This book will at-

TABLE 1.2 The 3 × 3 Curriculum Matrix at Work in Schools

Curriculum	Formal	Informal	Hidden
Written	Curriculum guides Textbooks	Tracking plans	Lived rules
Taught	Content taught (instruction)	Personality variables of the teacher	Authority role of the teacher
Tested	Standardized tests Teacher tests	Test behavior	Cultural norms Socioeconomic status

tempt to integrate all these versions of the "curriculum" to help school administrators use the power of a fused approach in improving pupil learning in schools.

1.6 Conventional Practices and Complaints About Curriculum

Conventional practices concerning curriculum include that it is "developed" or created by teachers to assist them in identifying commonalities to teach within local and state policies. School curriculum is supposed to be independent of textbook adoption so that, in theory, the textbook does not come to replace curriculum but is instead a means of implementing it.

Conventional ideas about curriculum include that it is the epitome of local control of the "content" of teaching, is responsive to local demands and priorities, and optimizes the peculiar interests and strengths of the teaching staff. It is supposed to have been created by writing a philosophy first and then filtering goals and other priorities through a tripartite data base of social needs, knowledge requirements, and the tenets of learning psychology. This approach has been called the "Tyler Rationale" (Tyler, 1949).

A. *Problem 1: Curriculum Clutter*

There isn't a veteran teacher or administrator who hasn't at some point in his or her career come to the conclusion that there is simply "too much" in the curriculum to teach, and a whole lot of it doesn't seem to be related.

The U.S. public school curriculum is replete with fragmentation, "itsy-bitsy" desiderata that, taken together, represent a kind of "crazy quilt" of topics and subjects. Such a curriculum lacks coherence and focus. It is extremely difficult to set priorities because each "piece" has a priority all its own. Furthermore, each segment has vested political interests behind it to ensure it remains "in" the curriculum.

The lack of a "grand design" in the U.S. school is the result of the extreme decentralization of curriculum practice over a long period of time (see Kliebard, 1986). Curriculum is "developed" at the national level in the form of textbook publishing and test use, at the state level with state guidelines and tests, and at the local level with local board priorities mixed in with local teacher autonomy.

Weaving in and out of these three levels are various movements and "reform cycles" that bring in new ideas and "subjects" and, when dead, leave a bit of residue in the overall curriculum quilt (see Tanner & Tanner, 1990). These movements are often antithetical to one another, which reinforces the tendency to fragment and segment them inside schools. It's the only way they can be "contained" and extended without inviting chaos.

The only way curriculum reformers can work in refocusing the U.S. curriculum is to step outside of it, because there is no sense in searching for a rationale that is internal to it to serve as a philosophy or theoretical umbrella to bring it together.

Examples of this type of approach would be Mortimer Adler's (1982) *The Paideia Proposal* or William Bennett's (1988) *American Education: Making It Work*. The problem with using an external rationale is that the values that support it are often not revealed or even stated. For example, Adler's rationale would eliminate all vocational education from the curriculum because he believes that it does not represent something of "timeless" value that would provide a "liberal" education. Adler does not envision vocational education as "liberal," a view that in some cases contrasts with historical facts; Plato himself in *The Republic* described an ideal curriculum as one comprising academics, aesthetics, and athletics.

In Plato's curriculum, there are no electives or cocurricular subjects. All three constitute a tripod of a whole curriculum that was based on the idea that the development of a human being had to involve the mind, the body, and the soul. Plato's elementary school curriculum comprised music and gymnastics. The secondary curriculum was centered on the military. Only in higher education were the academics finally pursued (see Pounds, 1968, pp. 40-41).

The lack of a coherent, rational approach to the conception of curriculum in U.S. education is foremost political; second, economic; and third, educational. The political divisions of federalism and the lack of a central ministry of education has meant that neither the government nor its political agents and agencies could define or enforce anybody's curriculum as overt policy. The economic issues relate to class and race divisions interspersed with socioeconomic position. Poor people historically have had very few options to select their schools or their curriculum.

Finally, as an educational issue, the education profession itself has been unable to come to terms with what ought to be taught or learned in U.S. schools for any length of time. The void has largely been filled by the textbook publishers.

The solution to curriculum clutter is to engage in the development of an overall rationale or philosophy that helps develop the boundaries to examine the age-old question, "What is worth putting in a school's curriculum?" This issue will be dealt with in Chapter 2.

B. *Problem 2: The Influence of Testing*

The phenomenon of testing has continued to expand in recent times. As the individual states have adopted various types of statewide measures and the scores on these instruments are made public, the impact of testing has become more pervasive in identifying what is of most worth to teach or learn. The answer has become, almost by default, in the absence of any larger rationale, *whatever the test is assessing*. So tests and test makers have come to occupy a primary role in defining curriculum content because it is quite natural to want to do "well" on the tests by making sure students have been taught what they need to know on them.

Thus "teaching to the test" not only make sense, it becomes a matter of survival. Pedagogically, there is nothing wrong with teaching to the test. Philosophically, however, there are a number of limitations that will be explored in Chapter 3 of this book.

c. Problem 3: Site-Based Management and Decentralization of Curriculum Development

U.S. education has swung from centralization to decentralization and back over a long time period (see Kliebard, 1986). The current emphasis on site-based management proposes to "empower" principals, teachers, parents, and students at schools to create more effective programs and procedures to educate children who are attending school there (Bailey, 1991).

If curriculum development is site based, then testing should also be site based, because in that manner schools can be held accountable for the "match" between the two. If this is not the case, then curriculum development creates content not a part of any testing scenario. Test scores will fall due to lost alignment.

To improve pupil test performance, it is necessary to improve the match between curriculum content and test content. This means "tightening" the relationship between what becomes the written curriculum, the taught curriculum, and its "alignment" to the tested curricula.

That relationship has been called "quality control" (English, 1978). It is shown in Figure 1.2.

Quality control means that, with specific actions, a target or goal (the written curriculum) becomes the basis for defining the work to be done (teaching), and both of these in turn are part of (aligned to) the tested curriculum. An administrator can "tighten"

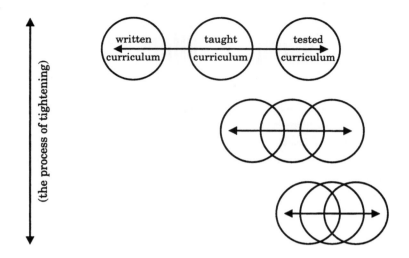

Figure 1.2. Quality Control in Curriculum Development

in any one of three ways. But "tightening" does not work unless all three are correlated (aligned).

Site-based management is a workable solution as a way to optimize the selection of methods or means at the local school level to optimize the "match" in quality control, because it is at this level where "teaching" is actually delivered.

D. *Problem 4: Loosely Coupled Systems and Teacher Autonomy*

Educational systems and the schools within them are not tightly interconnected. There is a great deal of "slack" between individual schools and the larger school system. Many contemporary critics propose cutting the individual schools "loose" from the system itself for all but the most perfunctory of duties (Maxcy, 1991). Whether or not this strategy is successful in improving pupil achievement, however, is in part a function of how success is measured.

If tests are used that presuppose a cumulative curriculum taught systematically over the years and across school buildings, then site-based management will not improve scores on these instruments because the "cumulative" impact of focused teaching is jeopardized. If each school becomes a school district, curricula sequence is often sacrificed. What is gained as a short-term benefit from being "liberated" from a highly bureaucratic and centralized system is lost as test scores fall.

Even if one takes steps to tighten the relationships between schools (curriculum articulation), the simple fact that schools in most school districts now are only minimally related one to the other presents barriers of geographic and physical dimensions of considerable magnitude. Much tradition has to be overcome in improving the correlation between the written, taught, and tested curricula due to the tradition of "loosely coupling."

The major avenue open to school districts regarding "tightening" (or quality control) is to tighten only in areas where it is required and not in every curricular area. These steps will be discussed in detail in Chapter 2.

Teacher autonomy presents problems to administrators in terms of adequate supervision and monitoring. There really is no way to observe teachers and adjust the curriculum in a direct one-on-one manner because teachers only have a small "piece" of the total curriculum; observation is always obtrusive and changes the classroom room environment; and principals can't be present for a very long time given the excessive spans of control most must live with in the day-to-day operations of their schools.

For these reasons, modern supervision and monitoring depend to a large extent on getting teachers to monitor themselves and "training" teachers to follow the curricular materials published by the local or state agencies involved. The more difficult the testing scenario is, the more district officials may resort to the publication of materials that become more detailed and often more routinized.

Such practices have the effect of "deskilling" teachers (Apple, 1979). The simple fact is that, the more tests are used to calibrate the success of learning in schools (and, by inference, of teaching), the more curricular materials are developed to focus (and thus limit) the viable options teachers may select. The use of any materials, however, ultimately has a similar impact.

The important question is this: Are the limitations consciously imposed after deliberate decision making, or are they imposed by system requirements? If the intervention is by system requirements, school districts have a special obligation to fully explore the hidden issues at work in the development of curricula that focus the work of teachers in classrooms. The real question is then: "Focusing by whom to obtain what for whom?" The heart of that question involves considering who the real clients of the schools are (children or society) and who is working for whom (teachers for administrators, for society, for children, or for themselves; see Courts, 1991).

E. *Problem 5: The Deadening Impact of Textbooks*

"The writing in most textbooks, particularly in the elementary textbooks, is choppy and stilted," notes Harriet Bernstein (1985, p. 464). She blames "states and cities that have mandated the use of readability formulas to determine the level of difficulty of a text." The use of such formulas makes the books harder rather than easier to read because it robs them of "connective tissue" that makes comprehension possible (see also Shannon, 1988).

Textbooks became a "fact of life" for U.S. schools after the Revolutionary War. Noah Webster sold his "spellers" from horseback and was perhaps the first to become wealthy from the sale of schoolbooks. His spellers were popular because they provided a curriculum to follow. U.S. schools in the nineteenth century were called a kind of organized anarchy, and the only thing that held them together was the textbooks used in them (Perkinson, 1985, p. x). But the domination of textbooks led to materials that appealed to the lowest common denominator among tastes and resulted in a "watered down curriculum" and progressively easier and more bland content (Perkinson, 1985, p. xi).

The stranglehold of textbooks in U.S. schools continues. Goldstein (1978) has estimated that at least 75% of a pupil's classroom time involves the use of a textbook. These data suggest that the most important curriculum decision a district's officials may make is not which curriculum to "develop" but which textbooks to adopt. No other work plan in a school exercises the dominant and profound influence of school textbooks.

1.7 The Necessary Requirements of an Effective Curriculum

To be effective in schools, a curriculum must have at least three essential characteristics. As a work plan, a curriculum must provide for *consistency* (or coordination). It must provide for *continuity* (or articulation). A curriculum must also provide for *flexibility* in adaptation as teachers interact with students. *Flexibility* means that the curriculum must be open to some interpretations in terms of how and under what classroom circumstances the content is most optimally taught. This means that the curriculum must be capable of being changed by altering the sequencing and pacing of its delivery *without* fundamentally altering its design fidelity.

The reason is that, with a work plan, the teacher is confronted with a range of differences in learners that eludes one of the most critical variables in planning any work activity, that is, *the absolute differences in the inputs* going into the work design itself.

From this perspective, the use of any manufacturing model in schools ultimately fails because nearly all operate on the assumption that somehow inputs can be *standardized*. With human beings, such an idea is absurd. Education cannot only not standardize people, but, if education is effective, it leads to greater differences between students, not less. Thus effective education quickly becomes destandardized in practice. Much of school ideology is aimed at "controlling" students by minimizing the differences between them, even as instruction is accentuating those same differences.

Effective school curriculum never attempts to standardize students but must, as a work plan, provide for focus and connectivity (coordination and articulation) *without* leading to slavish conformity where every teacher has exactly the same lesson on the same day from the same page in the same textbook. Such a situation would be profoundly unproductive and ineffective.

Curriculum in schools will always be in a state of tension between those requirements that are aimed at ensuring some sort of common content for all and those requirements that demand differences in approach, methods, and materials to attain the common outcomes.

If common outcomes are required, the curriculum must enable teachers within schools to mix methods and materials very differently to come anywhere near close to ensuring the learning of those desired commonalities. Differences have to be allowed in order to consider what is an expectation for all. What that means for curriculum development is that, *as a process,* it must define the necessary levels of focus and connectivity without leading to standardization.

Human variability defies the use of manufacturing/production models in schools. Yet schools exist to create some sort of social consensus about the perpetuation of a common life mode for everyone. Schools cannot let everyone "do their own thing" or there would be no school. On the other hand, schools cannot force everyone to do the same thing without jeopardizing their function in a society that contains, sustains, and protects those very same differences among its peoples. That is the challenge that faces educators involved in designing and delivering curriculum in the nation's schools.

Key Terms and Concepts

The following are definitions for the terms used throughout this book.

❏ *The curriculum.* The *curriculum* is the work plan or plans developed by or for teachers to use in classrooms by which the content, scope, and sequence of that content, and to some extent the methodology of their teaching, is defined and configured.

❏ *Instruction.* When teaching is influenced by or "guided by" a work plan (or curriculum), it becomes *instruction.* Instruction is focused and connected teaching. It is systematized teaching that adheres to the curriculum, and all formal testing scenarios (and tests) are implicitly based upon this teaching.

❑ *Coordination of curriculum.* This aspect of curriculum refers to the lateral or horizontal focus and connectivity of curriculum in a school environment. For example, a view of all ninth-grade algebra classes might reveal a common focus and connectivity present (though not necessarily identical). In this case, the curriculum is said to be "coordinated."

❑ *Articulation of curriculum.* When a curriculum is "articulated," it is focused and connected vertically from one grade to the next or from one school to the next. Another synonym for *articulation* is *continuity. Consistency* is a synonym for *coordination.*

❑ *Curriculum evaluation.* Evaluation of a curriculum may consist of assessing whether or not children have learned that which the curriculum indicated should be taught or it may be an assessment of the teacher in the act of delivering the curriculum. The latter is sometimes called *teacher evaluation.*

❑ *Design and delivery of curriculum.* The *design* of the curriculum refers to the act of creating it via specification or template. A *template* is simply the criteria or requirements a curriculum must fulfill or include. These might include state law, state testing, national goals, local priorities, and a specific learning theory or grouping practice.

Curriculum *delivery* refers to the act of implementing the curriculum. This may include teaching, monitoring, supervising, or the reconnecting of test data back to the curriculum so it reflects changes brought about by identified shortcomings from the test.

❑ *Curriculum alignment.* Curriculum *alignment* refers to the "match" or fit between the curriculum (in whatever form it may exist) and the test or tests to be used to assess learners. This is called *design alignment* because it is usually built into the curriculum as it is being developed.

Curriculum alignment also may refer to whether the teacher is teaching the curriculum and/or teaching to the test. If the curriculum and the test are aligned in the design stage of curriculum development, then a teacher will always teach to the test. If this does not occur, then the teacher may be teaching to the curriculum but not necessarily teaching to the test.

There is nothing wrong in teaching to the test if the test "matches" the objectives contained in the curriculum designed for delivery. In cases where tests are to be used as accurate and valid measures for determining whether pupil learning has occurred as intended, one always teaches to the test. If this were not the case, then test data would not have much to do with any specific curriculum and would be useless as a source of information to improve learning.

❏ *Curriculum auditing.* A *curriculum audit* is an external evaluation of the extent to which a school or school district's curriculum is being adequately managed to produce the desired learner outcomes within the fiscal and legal constraints in which a school system must function (English, 1988). Curriculum audits use five standards by which data are gathered from document reviews, interviews, and site visitations clustered around bench marks dealing with system control, direction, equity and consistency, use of feedback, and productivity (Steffy, 1989-1990).

❏ *Curricular quality control.* Quality control is a process that concerns the internal capability of a school system to improve its performance over time. It does this by developing goals and objectives (targeted behaviors), employing people to reach the goals (by striving to reach the targeted behaviors), periodically assessing the differences between desired and actual performance, and then using the discrepancy data to adjust and improve day-to-day operations.

Over time and with multiple adjustments in operations (teaching, grouping, testing), learner achievement improves as teaching becomes nearly identical to the "target behaviors" or objectives. The application of quality control is iterative in nature.

In schools, the elements are (a) the written curriculum (statement of the desired or targeted behaviors or outcomes), sometimes called the *work plan*; (b) the taught curriculum (the content the teacher teaches), sometimes called the *work*; and (c) the tested curriculum (that which is involved with work measurement as either teacher performance assessment or learner evaluation).

❏ *"Tightening" the curriculum.* This idea refers to actions that bring the written, taught, and tested curricula into alignment or congruence with one another. *Tightening* means that the lack of overlap between the three curricula is decreased.

❏ *Data disaggregation.* The act of taking test items and breaking them into smaller components, skills, knowledge, and content for teaching in smaller pieces and from which to adjust the curriculum or the work plan so that teaching changes as a result. Such changes may include or exclude different content, may spend more time on certain areas to teach, and may alter the scope and/or sequence of curricular content.

❏ *Reconnecting data to the curriculum or "the reconnect."* Once test or assessment data have been disaggregated, they must be "reconnected" to the work plan so that teachers have a different set of directions from which to teach. The *reconnect* means that test information is attached back into the curriculum, and the curriculum is altered accordingly.

❏ *Frontloading.* This refers to the concept of design alignment in which the curriculum and the test(s) are "matched". One would begin the matching process by first writing the curriculum and then selecting, adapting, or developing the test that "fits" the curriculum (or is aligned with it). To engage in "frontloading," an entire curriculum must be developed before alignment to any test can occur. This means that "frontloading" is the most time-consuming and expensive way to establish alignment.

❏ *Backloading*. This means that one engages in alignment by beginning with the test and working "back" to the curriculum. In this case, the test developers are also the persons who write the curriculum. The major advantage to backloading is that it is quick and relatively inexpensive compared with the "frontloading" process. The reason is that an entire curriculum does not have to be written *before* alignment can take place.

There are several problems with "backloading" in that tests may not always measure the most important things to be taught or may measure something that in the judgment of the teacher should not be taught at the point of assessment. Furthermore, if the purpose of the test is to classify learners in some way prior to instruction taking place, backloading may assist in the process of misclassification.

If a school or school district cannot "frontload" their curriculum, however, because the state mandates the test to be used (they therefore cannot select the most appropriate test to match their local curriculum), the only real decision is whether to backload or not.

❏ *Content and context alignment*. Alignment between the test and the curriculum occurs at two levels. The first is called *content alignment* and refers to the situation where the test content and the curriculum content are the same. The second, *context alignment* (sometimes called *format* alignment), means that the testing protocol or scenario is the same as the one in the curriculum or work plan (textbook).

❏ *The rational system*. The idea here is that school systems are goal driven and the resources required to run them should be configured in such a way as to enable them to accomplish the desired or designated objectives. Organizations whose operations are directed by the desire to attain goals are called *rational* (Silver, 1983, p. 77). Curriculum management assumes that school systems are rational in nature.

References

Adler, M. J. (1982). *The Paideia proposal*. New York: Macmillan.

Apple, M. W. (1979). *Ideology and curriculum*. London: Routledge & Kegan Paul.

Aronowitz, S., & Giroux, H. A. (1985). *Education under siege*. South Hadley, MA: Bergin & Garvey.

Bailey, W. J. (1991). *School-site management applied*. Lancaster, PA: Technomic.

Bennett, W. J. (1988). *American education: Making it work.* Washington, DC: Government Printing Office.

Bernstein, B. (1990). *The structuring of pedagogic discourse: Class, codes, and control.* London: Routledge, Chapman & Hall.

Bernstein, H. T. (1985, March). The new politics of textbook adoption. *Phi Delta Kappan, 66*(7), 463-465.

Courts, P. L. (1991). *Literacy and empowerment.* South Hadley, MA: Bergin & Garvey.

English, F. W. (1978). *Quality control in curriculum development.* Arlington, VA: American Association of School Administrators.

English, F. W. (1987). *Curriculum management.* Springfield, IL: Charles C Thomas.

English, F. W. (1988). *Curriculum auditing.* Lancaster, PA: Technomic.

English, F. W., & Hill, J. C. (1990). *Restructuring: The principal and curriculum change.* Reston, VA: National Association of Secondary School Principals.

Goldstein, P. (1978). *Changing the American schoolbook.* Lexington, MA: D. C. Heath.

Hall, E. T. (1977). *Beyond culture.* Garden City, NY: Anchor.

Kliebard, H. M. (1986). *The struggle for the American curriculum 1893-1958.* Boston: Routledge & Kegan Paul.

Lortie, D. C. (1975). *School teacher.* Chicago: University of Chicago Press.

Maxcy, S. J. (1991). *Educational leadership.* South Hadley, MA: Bergin & Garvey.

Perkinson, H. J. (1985). American textbooks and educational change. In D. Svobodny (Ed.), *Early American textbooks 1775-1900* (pp. ix-xv). Washington, DC: Government Printing Office.

Pounds, R. L. (1968). *The development of education in Western culture.* New York: Appleton-Century-Crofts.

Schubert, W. H. (1980). *Curriculum books.* Washington, DC: University Press of America.

Shannon, P. (1988). *Broken promises: Reading instruction in twentieth-century America.* South Hadley, MA: Bergin & Garvey.

Silver, P. (1983). *Educational administration.* New York: Harper & Row.

Steffy, B. E. (1989-1990). Curriculum auditing as a state agency tool in takeovers of local school districts. *National Forum of Applied Educational Research Journal, 3*(1), 93-104.

Tanner, D., & Tanner, L. (1990). *History of the school curriculum.* New York: Macmillan.

Tyler, R. W. (1949). *Basic principles of curriculum and instruction.* Chicago: University of Chicago Press.

Weick, K. E. (1978, December). Educational organizations as loosely coupled systems. *Administrative Science Quarterly, 23,* 541-552.

2

A Template for Curriculum Construction

Curriculum development means that the school creates, adapts, or adopts various kinds of work plans for teachers to use to focus and connect their work in schools. As such, curriculum development includes the process of *textbook adoption* or the adoption of any other kind of document or material that exerts some shaping influence on what teachers choose to do in their classrooms.

When classroom teaching is influenced by these materials, it becomes *instruction*. Instruction is simply *systematized teaching*, which includes a single teacher but links all teachers together in some form of common purpose within a common curriculum core or content area (see Wallace, 1981).

The extent of commonality or connectedness is determined by the amount of "tightening" required to bring together the written, taught, and tested curricula to attain desired learner outcomes.

2.1 The Traditional View of Developing Curriculum

The traditional view of developing curriculum in schools is shown in Figure 2.1. The process begins with something called *needs assessment* (Kaufman & English, 1979). From this, goals or targets are developed that must be broken down into smaller, more tangible and measurable "chunks," called *objectives*.

Because most school curricula are organized around "subjects," the objectives have to be loaded into these clusters and located in schools, grouped into grades and courses, and within grades and courses further broken down into units and finally classroom lessons (see Ellis, Mackey, & Glenn, 1988, pp. 76-98).

Lessons are subject to tests of students, and from these measurements results are obtained, reanalyzed, and fed back into the needs assessment cycle, which is repeated until test results and learner outcomes are identical. This is what is meant by "meeting the needs" of students.

A. *The Ideology of the Curriculum Development Cycle*

Curriculum development used to be considered to be a special kind of "engineering" (see Beauchamp, 1975). Today, it is generally recognized that curriculum development is very much a "value-laden" process that in no way resembles a neutral activity akin to engineering. Any kind of activity in schools must be judged not only by what its stated purposes may be (like developing curriculum) but also by what it is doing compared with the unstated purposes of schooling.

It is to the area of the unstated purposes of schooling that much criticism of curriculum development has been aimed in

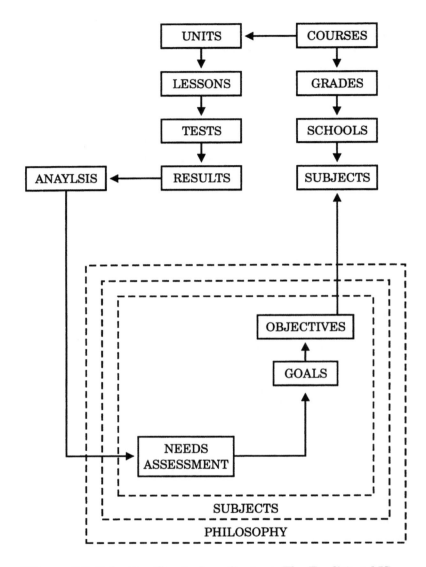

Figure 2.1. Selecting Curriculum Content: The Traditional View
NOTE: This is an ideology: a closed system.

recent times (see McLaren, 1986). For example, if schools are
conceptualized as places of opportunity for all children to climb
the ladder to "the good life" in America, school curricula may be

seen as liberating, with its focus on finding and exploiting native abilities.

On the other hand, if schools are viewed as vicious sorting machines that are racially and sexually biased places, reinforcing such biases in the larger society (Bowles & Gintis, 1976), then any curriculum that did not act contrary to these views would be also racially and sexually biased.

A view of curriculum development that is insensitive to these larger issues is naive. The creation of work plans in schools reinforces *something*. To know what that "something" actually is requires an educator to look carefully at what is really going on in schools, not only at their stated purposes and public rhetoric but at their hidden functions and unstated purposes. This is also a similar type of criticism regarding reform. If school reformers are not aware of the hidden functions of schools, they may not reform anything at all by making changes in them (Katz, 1987).

B. *The Myth of "Out There," Objective Knowledge to Serve as Curriculum Content in Schools*

Figure 2.2 shows how most educators conceptualize the development of curriculum by creating a so-called philosophy. After constructing their "philosophy," they then select the knowledge that is consonant with that view. This approach is an example of "naive realism" (Lincoln & Guba, 1985, p. 37). The "naive realist" believes that there is only one "reality" that awaits discovery somewhere "out there." This outlook assumes there is only one interpretation possible of knowledge and that it is "good" for all time and places, irrespective of historical context. The current controversy over "Afrocentric" curriculum is a good example of a conflict over interpretation of "facts." Afrocentrists want to replace Eurocentrists. The battle is over one "right" view as opposed to another "right view" when both views are probably possible.

The traditional curriculum development cycle is largely an exercise in ideology, that is, reinforcing a closed system of beliefs and answers without ever seriously questioning them (O'Neill,

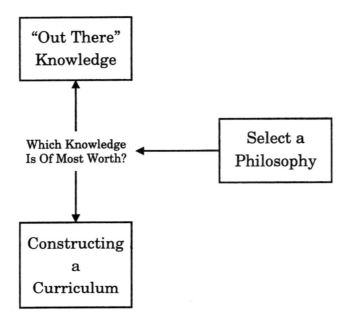

Figure 2.2. Selecting Curriculum Content: The Conventional View—"Naive Realism"

1981). The broken lines in Figure 2.1 represent these beliefs and answers as nonpublic and "hidden" values.

A needs assessment that functions within the unstated philosophy of school system operations and is centered in curriculum "subjects" is hardly an open-ended quest for truth. Instead, by being insensitive or oblivious to its own biases by not questioning them, it reinforces whatever they may be. A needs assessment cannot, therefore, be a truly open-ended search for values that may be selected by curriculum developers when some values are not stated or are "hidden" or are automatically selected a priori. This is why curriculum development traditionally conceptualized cannot be considered a "value-neutral" process like engineering.

The most common practice in developing curriculum is interested teachers being employed during a summer or after school hours to "write" curriculum. The teachers begin by identifying their "philosophy," which consists of listing their common "beliefs." Figure 2.2 is illustrative of this practice.

These statements may look something like:

"We believe all children can learn."

"We believe education should develop the whole child."

"We believe history should prepare students to live better in their world."

"We believe that critical thinking should be part of the curriculum."

Each of these statements is shrouded in values. For example, "we believe all children can learn" is a *tautology,* that is, true by definition. All children do learn in schools, though they may not learn what educators want them to or what is in the official curriculum. Human beings are learning all the time.

The statement "all children can learn" is akin to "all fish can swim." It reveals nothing and it predicts nothing. Yet it is commonly found throughout the literature of "effective schools" and appears in many schools' so-called philosophies (ideologies). A more accurate statement that would not be tautological might be this one: "All children can be successful in school."

The values embedded in the statement, "All children can be successful in school," are both overt and covert (hidden). The overt values are that, irrespective of background (socioeconomic level), race, or sex, it is believed that everyone can attain the indicators of achievement defined in the curriculum. No one is therefore excluded at the outset or excused from having to attain those outcomes. The overt value is egalitarian and encompassing. In practice, such a belief would challenge any procedure that "excused" some children from the same expectations indicated for "all children" for whatever reason.

At the same time, the *covert* values in the statement are that the "school," as it exists, is essentially correct for "all children" and that the burden is therefore on children to "adapt to" and "be successful" in them *as they exist.* Children therefore have to come to schools "ready" to learn in order to be successful in them. Parents have to ensure that their children are ready to learn. The "blame" for failure therefore rests squarely on the children and their parents, and not on the schools, if children don't learn in them.

That the school might not be "correct" is never considered in this context. If schools were to be accountable in this manner, the same statement might read, "All schools can be successful with all children" or "We believe that the school should be sufficiently flexible to be successful with all children." These statements would shift the locus of accountability from the students and their parents to the school and its staff.

Shifting the locus of accountability from the student to the school would make it more difficult for schools to behave in ways that have been clearly racist and sexist in enclaves in society. For example, a Texas superintendent once observed:

> You have doubtless heard that ignorance is bliss; it seems that it is so when one has to transplant onions. . . . If a man has very much sense or education either, he is not going to stick to this type of work. So you see it is up to the white population to keep the Mexican on his knees in an onion patch or in new ground. This does not mix very well with education. (Montejano, 1987, p. 193)

If the schools as they exist are left untouched or unexamined in the development of curriculum, then, whatever they do, and for whatever reason, remains unchanged. Curriculum development that does not challenge what schools do and how they do it is naive.

The development of the "whole child" incorporates a view that the school must be concerned with what the learner is feeling, the level of inner aspiration present, and the complete fabric of living and perceiving things. Such a belief transcends the idea that the school is mainly a repository of knowledge and is concerned only with passing that knowledge along in some acceptable mode. The "whole child" idea can be interpreted positively or negatively, depending upon one's perspective on it. For some politically conservative parents, the "whole child" concept is an intrusion into the "privacy" of the home. For other parents, it represents a posture that they may see as positive and caring for the sensitivities and feelings of their children while they spend time in an institutional environment for a part of their day (see Purpel, 1988).

The belief statement, "We believe history should prepare students to live better in their world," puts a twist on the approach to dealing with the past. This statement would shape the past and provide meaning primarily from the value stance of the current time. Current meanings are always undergoing change. For example, Christopher Columbus was seen as a courageous and inspirational explorer in the past. To many, under the standards of the current time, he was a cruel, exploitative, racist colonizer who helped exterminate native Indian tribes via torture and intimidation. Whose interpretation is to be used to teach who Christopher Columbus was to American schoolchildren (see Mitchell & Weiler, 1991)?

The "critical thinking" goal is quite common as a curricular "belief" statement in schools. Yet most social scientists studying schools would deny that teachers or administrators really desire students to think critically at all. No school teaches children to criticize the Ten Commandments or the assumptions that support them. No school would create a curriculum that even hinted at the notion that monogamy would not be preferred over polygamy (though polygamy is an acceptable practice in other cultures). Students are not taught in schools to be critical of the work they may be asked to perform in factories and offices after they graduate from school and enter the world of work (see Simon, Dippo, & Schenke, 1991). In the words of anthropologist Edward Hall (1977, p. 205), "School life is an excellent preparation for understanding adult bureaucracies: it is designed less for learning than for teaching you who's boss and how bosses behave, and keeping order."

Critical thinking usually narrowly refers to solving higher-order decontextualized mathematical problems, working in specified (but socially acceptable) art media, or working in one of the "hard" scientific disciplines like physics, chemistry, or in biology (sufficiently roped off to exclude dealing with the *theory of evolution*).

Critical thinking never means learning to be skeptical or truly critical of one's own cultural values and biases, the way the school is organized, what the teacher may choose to teach or the way he or she chooses to teach it, or school routines such as rigid adherence to schedules and routines (the "lived" curriculum).

Conventional curriculum practices largely ignore the questions of "whose values" should be propagated in the schools, and, because they are almost never questioned, the existing power relationships in the larger society into which schools fit are reinforced and extended by such practices. Figure 2.3 is illustrative of this point.

c. *Developing Curriculum Is a Political Act*

Knowledge is never neutral. The selection of knowledge to include in a school curriculum is *fundamentally a political act* of deciding who benefits from selecting what in the school's curriculum and who is excluded or diminished simultaneously.

A more accurate view of what is really going on in developing a curriculum is shown in Figure 2.4. Curriculum construction goes on in schools within the unspoken and dominant educational ideology: the dominant political ideology that serves as "hidden" screens for the actual process of writing the acceptable work plans in schools. Rarely are these screens made overt or completely understandable. For example, Shor (1986, pp. 104-194) avers that the national call for "excellence" and "high tech" are simply camouflaged strategies to maintain the existing political authority structure and inequality in the larger society.

The "we believe" statements commonly "guiding" curriculum construction in most school districts are nothing more than *ideological political screens* to ensure that whatever is finally "developed" conforms to the ideology. After this, knowledge or content (the so-called facts) is selected to match this screen.

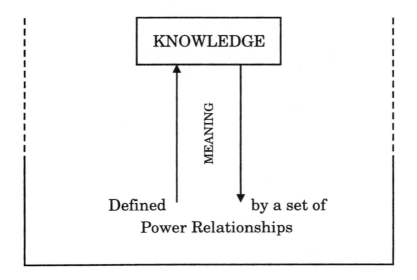

• Who benefits from this knowledge?

• Who is excluded from this knowledge?

Figure 2.3. Selecting Curriculum Content

Because this is never a truly open-ended process, the knowledge "selected" really has been preselected, preshaped to fit whatever the dominant cultural configuration happens to be at the time. When the process is passed off as "engineering" or "scientific," its real biases are submerged in a fake kind of "objective neutrality" that belies its essential subjectivity.

School curricula are almost never written from a philosophical base in day-to-day operations of local educational systems. At the state and national levels, in terms of problems in education, philosophy is rarely, if ever, applied. The reason is that true philosophy is highly abstract and quite generalized beyond a day-to-day arena of decision making or even a year-to-year one. Ideologies, on the other hand, as O'Neill (1981, p. 19) points out,

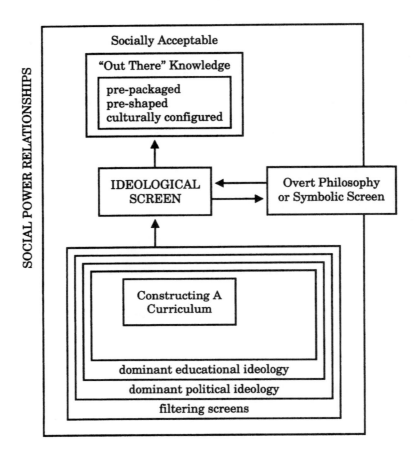

Figure 2.4. Selecting Curriculum Content: The More Accurate View

are much more specific and actually may direct social and political actions.

Because curriculum construction is aimed at directing educationally induced social and political actions, the outcomes are more accurately the product of an ideology as opposed to a philosophy. In addition, philosophies are much more apt to be concerned with processes and procedures as "protocols of inquiry" rather than a doctrine of belief. The "we believe's" of curriculum development are in fact statements of ideologies as opposed to philosophies.

2.2 Using a Needs Assessment to Develop a Curricular Framework

Curriculum development starts with a needs assessment, which is not a survey of faculty or parents about what they "need" in the schools. That kind of survey is merely a "perceptual inventory" of how people "feel" or "see" various programs and priorities that may or may not exist in the schools.

A needs assessment is a "gap analysis" of the *existing level of pupil performance* compared with *the desired level of pupil performance* (Kaufman & Herman, 1991, p. 140). To determine a need, the school administrator must have two indices present. The first is some tangible and measurable statement of outcomes that is valid and reliable. The second is a set of measurement instruments by which to assess the existing level of pupil performance compared with the desired levels. In neither case is a curriculum required, because valid and reliable indicators or objectives are part of but not a whole curriculum, and a set of measurement tools may be part of but not a whole curriculum.

Obtaining a set of valid and reliable outcomes by which a needs assessment is performed is the first task of the educator in constructing curriculum.

A. *Creating Valid and Reliable Educational Outcome Indicators*

Generating a comprehensive list of valid and reliable outcome indicators is the first task in performing a needs assessment. Outcome indicators are discrete learner performance statements that are "macro" level in scope; that is, they represent the more or less final point of where learners should be or what they should know, feel, or do when the responsibilities of the school system are officially over. That means the outcome indicators are for 12th grade plus in K-12 school systems. One way to think about it is that, when a student steps forward to receive his or her high school diploma, what are the minimally essential skills, knowledge, and attitudes that he or she should possess?

One example might be this one, "At the conclusion of the 12th grade, the student will be able to read the editorial page of *The New York Times* with 100% accuracy and be able to point out instances of arguments not based on logic or fact."

This statement is very different than one that simply asserts, "At the end of the 12th grade, students will be able to think critically." This type of outcome statement is too global to be of very much use in performing a needs assessment, because that process will require the selection of measurement tools to assess whether or not students can or do perform at the level required or implied in an outcome statement. If statements are as vague as the latter one, it is very hard to select an appropriate measurement tool or procedure. In such cases, the selection of the tool then really functions to define what was meant in the construction of the indicator. In this instance, the test or measurement tool becomes the indicator instead of independently measuring its attainment. For this not to happen, outcome indicators must be as specific as test content, or the test content becomes the substitute for the curriculum content and redefines the true meaning of the indicator itself.

B. *The Curriculum Outcome Indicator Validation Matrix*

The potential list of outcome indicators is nearly infinite, especially when one considers the limited amount of pupil time available for schooling, which is between 14,000 and 15,000 hours, K-12. The rate of knowledge known to human kind is doubling every two to five years, which increases the pressures on selecting indicators and subsequent content that are indeed "most valuable."

One method to select the most appropriate curriculum outcome indicators is to construct a curriculum outcome validation matrix. The matrix is shown in Table 2.1.

The matrix is simply a listing of groups or persons considered to be critical in determining agreement with any proposed set of outcome indicators. There can be as many as required or desired.

TABLE 2.1 A Sample Curriculum Content Validation Matrix

Proposed Content to Be Included in the Curriculum	State Law	National Task Force	State Test	Local Policy	Local Teacher Poll	Textbook	Futurists
Content (however defined)	Reference all applicable provisions of existing state law to the proposed content in this column.	Refer specifically to task force reports in content areas such as the NCTM, AAAS, NCTE, and the like.	Perform an initial review of the alignment of the content of the state test(s) and the proposed content for your curriculum.	Refer to relevant local policy requirements or adopted outcome goals.	This column can refer to priorities of teachers regarding possible content inclusion.	Reference existing and proposed textbook content to proposed content in this column.	Use selected futurists to establish trends that your graduates will face.
Skills							
Attitudes							
Processes							
Concepts							
Other							

The listing under the "proposed content" column can be in any form desired so long as it is specific enough to relate to the references and the tests that will be used to assess them. The outcome indicators can be in the form of content to be learned or processes, skills, attitudes, or concepts to be acquired.

In this context, *validation* means simply the attainment of consensus of the referent groups or persons used in the matrix. School officials will have to set the level of consensus; that is, how many "yes" or "matches" actually constitute consensus and whether all groups/persons are counted with the same weight.

The most common referents used in curriculum validation are state law and regulations, state tests, local board policies or requirements, textbook references, national curricular task forces, recommendations from national educational curriculum organizations (such as the National Council of Teachers of Mathematics or the National Council of Teachers of English), local teachers, and futurists.

Futurists are an important source to validate proposed curriculum outcome indicators if educators argue that the curriculum will prepare students to function in a world that as yet does not exist. Such futurists identify key trends that will have an impact on the lives of the students in their times.

For example, if the next century is the "Asian Century" as so many predict, with the locus of the world's development shifting to the Pacific Rim, what should school curricula include to prepare students to work in this world? (See Cetron & Gayle, 1991, pp. 93-128.) The answer is not simple because it is influenced by one's "ideology." If the curriculum developer is a political conservative, he or she may simply say: "Educate a student in the basic liberal arts and he or she will know how to confront any situation." If a curriculum developer is more liberal, he or she may say, "Asian culture and the Japanese language should replace the heavy emphasis on the European culture and Latin."

Actually, the curriculum matrix proposes an eclectic response in which all of the opinions are factored into making this determination.

It should be noted, however, that almost all available sources are politically and educationally conservative in outlook. Citizen polls, state legislatures, national task forces, and tests as well as boards of education will reflect a dominant emphasis on the status quo or the past, because that is the frame of reference of most of the respondents in the matrix. Emerging social needs usually run far ahead of the perception of those working in schools, which helps explain why much of the curriculum is outdated. A standing joke in social studies is that it is nearly always "one war behind."

Once the validation matrix is constructed, and the groups and persons are invited to indicate their agreement or disagreement, then the results are tabulated. Each person or group is allowed one vote (a "yes" or a "no" vote). The level of agreement may be set at 90%, in which case a level of consensus that is lower than that would not be considered for inclusion into a school or school district's list of outcome indicators. Respondents may "rank" the potential outcome indicators on several scales connoting importance. In this case, numerical averages are computed to show high and low ones as an index of perceived group and overall importance.

It should be noted that the development of these general district indicators is not located within any particular curriculum content area; that is, they do not represent a discipline so that the indicators are "out of discipline." Curriculum content areas (math, science, language arts, and so on) are simply convenient grouping points or "organizing centers" for curriculum content considered similar or comparable.

If one only develops outcome indicators in math, for example, the inclusion of "math" is a foregone conclusion in the subsequent development of curriculum. This option also forecloses locating an outcome indicator in some other area of the curriculum that may be more appropriate.

For example, "balancing a checkbook" could be ranked as an outcome indicator in math. Or it could be an indicator in home economics or even social studies. Once it is ranked as a "math" outcome indicator, however, the option for locating it elsewhere may be foreclosed.

For curriculum developers to have maximum latitude to locate outcome indicators in the most appropriate content area, outcome indicators should be listed initially without regard to the curriculum discipline in which they traditionally may be found.

c. Selecting the Measurement Tools to Determine Pupil Performance

Remembering that a needs assessment is a gap analysis between the desired level of pupil performance and the actual level of performance, pupil attainment must now be assessed in relationship to the outcome indicators.

What this means is that a test or tests must be selected that really match the outcome indicators so that a score derived from the test is considered an appropriate measure of the actual level of pupil learning on a specific outcome indicator.

Tests therefore have to be aligned with the outcome indicators. A combination of tests and other types of assessments can be used as well as homegrown tests to determine how well pupils have learned that which is required for them to do well on the outcome indicators.

In some cases, the outcome indicators will have to be broken down into smaller pieces and tested at grade levels earlier than the 12th grade. The process of defining the outcome indicators into smaller components is largely one of logical extrapolation in which the requisite subskills and knowledge are delineated (see Glatthorn, 1987, pp. 143-159).

Test reliability is generally known for commercially prepared batteries and to some extent for statewide instruments. For locally developed criterion-referenced tests or teacher-made tests, reliability will have to be established. Although there are several forms of determining test reliability, the Kuder-Richardson test item approach is a standard procedure often used for this purpose (see Payne, 1968, pp. 129-140). Computer programs for using the KR-20 are available for purchase and use in school systems.

Once the tests and other assessments have been given to the students and the scores compiled, then the actual needs assessment process can begin. The needs assessment is simply a list of gaps or discrepancies between desired and actual levels of pupil performance in a school or a school district.

Gaps or "needs" are usually listed by size and by indicator priority. For example, suppose 29% of the students could not read and interpret that editorial in *The New York Times*. That gap may not be as important as noting that 42% of the graduating seniors could not recognize the opening strains of Beethoven's *Fifth Symphony*. Although the music "need" is larger, it may not have the same importance as the one in reading and interpretation of expository prose.

2.3 Constructing Curriculum With Gap Data

The gap or "need" data can be used to construct or adapt a curriculum. Remembering that a curriculum is a type of work plan, the discrepancy data can be attached to places in the existing curriculum or textbook series where skills, knowledge, and attitudes are supposed to be taught. This act simply reconnects the needs assessment data back to the work plan in whatever form it exists. As the curriculum constructors examine the reconnection, they should be searching to see whether the learning discrepancies are the result of inadequacies in the work plan.

For example, suppose that, in trying to improve the number of students who can read *The New York Times* properly, the curriculum developers discover that the curriculum has very few examples like the one outcome indicator on which they are being tested. By moving to expand this area in the curriculum, they ensure that many more students may pass that item on subsequent tests. The alteration of the work plan is part of cur- └ based on gap data
riculum development.

In case there is no work plan of any kind, a curriculum is constructed by arraying the outcome indicators and their requisite subskills into the logical descending order to be taught. In this way, needs assessment data that are largely *descriptive* become a *prescription*. If such subskills and knowledge are to be

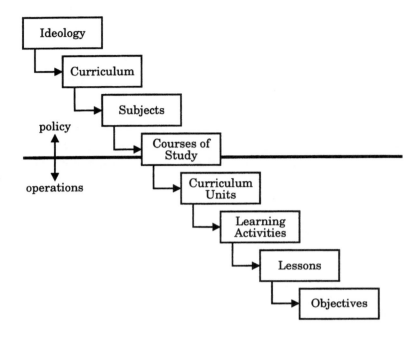

Figure 2.5. Traditional Curriculum Development Sequence

taught repetitively in greater sophistication with subsequent grades, a spiral curriculum is the result. Repetition in teaching is not only a function of ensuring mastery (a delivery concern) but of building into the curriculum the necessary reinforcement (a curriculum design problem; see Gagne & Briggs, 1979).

Figure 2.5 shows the progression of curriculum development generally followed in many school systems. Beginning with the construction of an ideology and the derivation of outcome indicators and subsequent tests, gaps become the basis of the construction of curriculum (the needs assessment). In turn, revealed gaps are located in curricular subjects and then in courses of study. From these, smaller divisions of curriculum called *units* are created. Within units, learning activities, objectives, and lesson plans carry the development of a detailed work plan to the classroom teacher to deliver (see McNeil, 1977, pp. 93-103).

2.4 Constructing "User Friendly" Curriculum Work Plans

The legends about curriculum guides being "Manhattan tele-phone books," gathering dust in classroom corners and closets, are legion in the teaching profession. A veteran principal once commented to me, "I've been in the Fort Worth Independent School District for 40 years, and in all that time nobody ever stole a curriculum guide!" This anecdote epitomizes the lack of true utility such work plans often have for classroom teachers. They are ponderous and of dubious validity. Often they are not much more than "cut-and-paste" old textbooks that were glued together to satisfy the requirements for a little curriculum work for a couple of weeks of afternoon summer speculation. Why school districts continue to pay scarce taxpayer dollars for the construction of materials that are of marginal worth to the im-provement of pupil learning remains one of the enduring myster-ies of education. Perhaps they don't know any better. To improve the quality of curricular work plans, we must examine some of the regnant myths about them.

A. *Myth 1: "Bubble-Up" Curriculum Approaches Are Best to Ensure Teacher Loyalty*

One of the great fallacies that permeates the curriculum field is the notion about the requirement for teachers to develop their own curriculum or work plans. The rationale goes that, if they don't actually write it, they don't or won't "own it," and if they don't "own it," it will all come to naught (see Taba, 1962, p. 469).

This myth ignores the fact that most teachers are far more loyal to their textbooks than to curriculum guides, even when they wrote the guides. Teacher loyalty is given to those materi-als that really *work with children*. The matter of who wrote them is quite secondary. The bulk of materials used by most teachers is material they did not write themselves. It is, how-ever, quite true that, while teachers may not have written their work plans, they have considerable leeway in selecting those they feel are effective with their children. That is an important point. Ownership means making a personal decision about "what works" and having the professional power to keep using those things that work and to expand them.

B. *Myth 2: Teachers Alone Know the Secrets of What Is Best for Children*

Much of the curriculum literature is filled with pictures of teachers pondering the future of the world, working to develop curriculum that helps children move into the future. The fact is that teachers work under an enormous set of constraints in developing curriculum.

The intrusion of state law and new requirements most often in the form of mandates for subject matter or sequencing; state testing programs that are politically motivated and administered to reveal "deficit schools or school systems," of which, by definition, nearly 50% are conceded to be at the outset by the logic of the statistical machinery employed; and textbook adoptions that also standardize the curriculum—all must somehow be taken into account.

To develop a curriculum that ignores these powerful forces would be to create an irrelevant document few actually referenced. So teachers cannot act in isolation in developing curriculum. They must acknowledge the power and influence other groups in U.S. society possess in setting the context in which curriculum development is undertaken. The authorization of teachers to write curriculum always occurs within a specified legal-social-political context in which schools must function.

Although teachers work most days with the same children, this familiarity may not be translated to the development of effective curriculum or work plans. Writing a kind of work plan that is easily followed by someone else takes a special kind of skill and communication ability. Great teaching may be in part improvisation backed with intuition. These two sources are not necessarily connected to writing intelligible documents other people can follow and attain similar results. Similar results from one setting to the other are involved with reliability, and clarity and specificity are very much related to this characteristic.

c. *Myth 3: Curriculum Should Be Developed Independently of Textbooks and Tests*

Traditionally, curriculum has been viewed as a separate kind of effort to produce a uniquely local work plan. The rationale is that localized curriculum should not be influenced by textbooks or tests. The notion is that curriculum should *lead* and *not follow*.

What is often forgotten in this approach is that, if a school or school district releases many different kinds of work plans to teachers, the designers have some obligation to determine which is the best and the intercorrelation between them. This should be a primary objective in the creation of work plans because teachers have the option of choosing which one to use in most cases.

On the other hand, once curriculum is seen as one of a number of different types of work plans that may exist in a school, then its relationships to the other work plans that may exist becomes an important consideration. The so-called primacy of localized curriculum usually only exists in the head of the superintendent or chief curriculum officer. Such primacy is often nonexistent out in the schools as textbooks continue to dominate classroom teaching as the major work plan (see Apple, 1986).

The other "myth" is that those who construct the curriculum should maintain a "blind eye" to what is tested. This posture prevents those constructing the work plan from understanding how and what will be measured. It would be similar to determining to build some kind of product and not having any idea of how the quality of the item would be assessed for fear that somehow the assessment process itself would somehow be damaged.

If the assessment is indeed measuring the desired work to be done, then the assessment criteria should be the same as for the item itself. The only way assessment data are useful to improve the actual work going on is through ensuring that the work being assessed is the work desired to be accomplished. These issues will be discussed in greater detail in Chapter 3 on alignment.

2.5 Moving From Curriculum Content to Work Tasks

After curriculum validation occurs, the next task is to transpose the most highly ranked content into a form that makes it easily translated into the classroom. This means that content must be stated in the form of work tasks for the teacher. A good way of thinking about this problem is to pose these questions:

- The teacher is to do what?
- Under what conditions?
- With what tools or materials?
- To attain what results?

Typically, many curriculum guides begin by stating the work tasks for the teacher as a "behavioral" objective (see Mager, 1962). This is a mistake. First, behavioral objectives are not statements of teacher work tasks, they are statements of *work measurement* (English, 1987, p. 193). Behavioral objectives indicate what students are to do, not what teachers should be teaching. If behavioral objectives are going to be used in a curriculum guide, they should be used in a section pertaining to evaluation (Armstrong, Cornell, Kraner, & Roberson, 1970).

The way to state teacher tasks is to focus on actions that the teacher should be taking with the specified content. For example:

> During a discussion of famous American women who were minorities, introduce the case of Lucy Gonzales Parsons, one of the first Chicanas to make a significant contribution to the American labor movement. Present the status of American labor in the late Nineteenth Century which led to the Haymarket Massacre. Show the students how Lucy Gonzales Parsons' work led to the establishment of the eight hour day. (Mirande & Enriquez, 1979, p. 88)

Another way to state the work of the teacher would be this: "Present the life of Lucy Gonzales Parsons as an exemplar of early American feminism among minorities. Have the students perform library research on her life and develop several vignettes for a small playlet for performance for the class."

Exactly how much detail should be present in a curriculum guide regarding teacher work tasks *depends* upon (a) the sophistication and knowledge of the staff, (b) the type of content that has been selected, (c) the extent of dependence of the staff upon access to critical facilities (labs, libraries, computers, and so on), (d) the presence and availability of appropriate materials such as textbooks and other supplementary materials, (e) the expectations of achievement as embodied in local, state, or national tests/exams, and (f) the range and diversity of the pupil population and any special requirements they may possess to engage in successful learning.

In one scenario, let us suppose that "School District A" is a rapidly growing but older school system near an inner city in the Southwest. There has been high teacher turnover and a large percentage of the faculty are newcomers to teaching. They meet students who are coming from poor neighborhoods with all the attendant problems associated with poverty. Although some of the school buildings are modern, they are not stocked well with books and supplementary materials. The state has recently initiated a testing program in which large numbers of students have performed poorly. If the poor pupil performance continues, the district faces possible sanctions.

The curriculum guide developed for School District A will contain much more explicit information for young, inexperienced faculty than if the faculty were seasoned and successful veterans. The guides will contain many more references that entail methodological work tasks (how to present something) than not. Connections from the content to the students will reference ways teachers can create materials not available to them because of the lack of adequate supplementary materials. And the presence of the state-imposed and mandatory testing program means that critical *alignment* information should be included in the guides to ensure maximum pupil performance. Guides should be rich with alignment data regarding examples of how students will be assessed and also show sample question formats. Recommended time ranges should be present to help an inexperienced faculty focus on the highest priorities with the students.

Now take "School District B." This is a wealthy suburban school system with experienced teachers who are quite stable. Likewise, the student population is very stable and well off. Scores on state tests are high and responsive to state criteria. The curriculum guide for School District B is likely to be leaner, smaller, and cryptic. It might even be in the form of a one-page checklist reminder format.

Functional work plans fit the situation. They enable the faculty to quickly focus on the essentials, make the necessary connections, relate essential learning to the school environment, and maximize pupil success, however locally defined.

2.6 Constructing "User Friendly" Curriculum Guides

"User friendly" curriculum guides emphasize the development of well-organized, easy to read, unambiguous textual language that is contextually relevant to real classrooms and real procedures. "Pie-in-the-sky" platitudes, elaborate philosophies, academic rhetoric or research mumbo jumbo, long lists of excessively technical performance objectives, numerous footnotes and quotations, and the like should be eliminated from functional work plans as they assume the form of a curriculum guide.

Textbook companies spend millions trying to perfect the process of translation from the book to the classroom. As a reminder, pick out a textbook that teachers in your building enjoy using and examine the *Teacher's Guide*. The probability is quite good that what you will see are "simple and lean" "user friendly" directions and examples that make it easy to move from a desired state to one present in a classroom. Modern textbooks might be vapid on content (a charge frequently heard), but they are far superior to any yet produced as examples of effective work plans that actually can *be taught as written.*

Functional curriculum guides take into account the work situation, the nature of the teachers and students, relevant expectations as embodied in law, and evaluation procedures (tests). They enable teachers to tie together the important elements of being "in control" of the classrooms in which they work.

"User friendly" curriculum guides are *stand-alone* documents; that is, they require no other document to understand, interpret, or refer to in order to "tighten" the curriculum (written, taught, and tested) if desired. "User friendly" curriculum guides are well indexed; cross referencing by topic and problem is easy. It is possible for a veteran teacher to "get into" and "get out of" a guide quickly and easily without having to read the whole thing.

"User friendly" curriculum guides are small. They fit into purses and pockets easily. They do not resemble huge, three-ring binders that discourage teachers from using them.

2.7 Essential Elements in Curriculum Guides

It is quite conceivable in some situations that all a curriculum guide might contain would be a listing of the required content to be taught (in whatever form the "content" assumes). That would be all that would be required in some circumstances where pupil performance was deemed to be adequate and no "tightening" was necessary.

What, however, can a district and its staff do if this is not the case? Suppose that a school district's test scores or other measures of academic learning are not deemed to be adequate. What can be done? If the district only has a checklist type of curriculum guide, the data base will not be adequate to improve pupil performance.

In this case, the district will have to reconstruct its work plans to enable it to more fully concentrate its resources to improve pupil performance. The purpose of a functional curriculum guide is to *focus* and *connect* the work of teachers.

Tests, no matter what kind and no matter where administered, *assume* some kind of common experience to be possible in some sort of sequence, or else a comparison of one score with another would be impossible. Test scores assume the presence of a continuous variable (see Allen & Yen, 1979, p. 20). Commonality is a necessary assumption that must be present to connote meaning in any score compared with another. If every test score were totally idiosyncratic (i.e., one time only and absolutely unique), it would be ludicrous to make judgments on the basis of comparisons. Tests will always be an important variable in constructing curriculum, whether they come *after* or *before* curriculum. (These options will be pursued in greater detail in the next chapter.)

The curriculum-test connection should be represented in a curriculum guide so that the classroom teacher knows what will be tested, when, and with what instruments. This connection can be as simple as that shown in Table 2.2, where "O" means a match with the tests, and "X" connotes a match with the curriculum and the test (this would be content alignment only).

A standardized norm-referenced test presents scores on the basis of how well a student performed compared with all of the other students who took a test. A criterion-referenced test reports a score on how many student answers were correct or incorrect. A common kind of criterion-referenced test many adults have taken and passed is the state driver's test.

From this sample of the 10 curricular objectives, the district's own criterion-referenced test would have the highest content alignment, followed by the state achievement test and the norm-referenced test. Teachers should know which tests will assess what curricular objectives *and the format that will be used to assess them* (context alignment). A detailed discussion regarding test ethics will be pursued in the next chapter.

The curriculum guide should indicate what should be taught (and also what will or should be learned), how what is to be taught or learned will be assessed, and by which instrument and when, and curricular objectives should be keyed to the textbooks teachers may use to implement the designated curricular objectives (by page number).

TABLE 2.2 Representing the Curriculum/Test Connection in Curriculum Guides

Curriculum Objective	Scope of Test Used		
	NRT	STATE CAP	DISTRICT CRT
1. Ability to infer the author's purpose, point of view, in a literary work	O	O	X
2. Ability to distinguish facts from normative statements	O	X	X
3. Can recognize cause-effect relationships	X	X	X
4. Can predict trends from given data	X	O	O
5. Can identify value judgments in various texts	O	O	X
6. Knowledge of early civilizations	X	X	O
7. Understands at least two nonmajority cultures in the United States	O	X	O
8. Ability to relate a story in personal terms	O	O	O
9. Can pick out logical fallacies in arguments	O	O	X
10. Can indicate from a TV advertisement various forms of propaganda in use	O	O	X
Totals	3	4	6

NOTE: NRT = the norm-referenced test used in the school system. STATE CAP = the state achievement test. DISTRICT CRT = the school system's criterion-referenced test.

The keying of the textbook and the curriculum in this fashion means that, as teachers are following the curriculum, they will be *moving around* the textbook and not teaching merely chapter 1, 2, 3, and 4 in that order. For curricula to dominate and lead textbooks, the essential data teachers require should be present in the most easily translatable form possible. Unless the textbook pages are present, most teachers will not take the time to look them up, finally putting the guide aside and following the sequence of the test instead of the sequence of the curriculum.

Many school systems are also placing videocassettes, audiocassettes, films, filmstrips, and other aides by topic in curriculum guides next to curricular objectives. In this way, teachers know very quickly not only where various curricular objectives can be located in all of the textbooks but also what other resources contain the curricular objectives that must be taught and learned.

Finally, there must be some sort of time designation within the curriculum guide as to how much stress (in some convenient unit of time) is required to teach the designated objectives (or topics, subjects, themes, facts, processes, or the like).

The time designation is a prickly issue with teacher committees. Teachers often are reluctant to designate any time at all for fear it will be turned around and employed as an evaluative tool against them. For example, if they indicate that two periods should be spent on "applying context clues to determine meaning" in literature, experience will indicate that some students will take less than two periods and many may take considerably more. What then is the value of the designation if not to evaluate teacher efficiency?

The value of the time designation is considerably enhanced if the time is represented as *ranges of time* instead of *fixed units*. When provided with ranges of time based on pupil learning, teachers can receive some idea of the overall emphasis to be obtained and gain some idea as to how long it should take them to teach a concept, process, skill, fact, or the like.

Work plans without time specifications are nearly useless in eliminating the near universal teacher complaint about homegrown curriculum guides: "There's too much to teach in too little time to teach it in." This is a rather simple time/work problem familiar to industrial engineers. What makes development of practical work plans very difficult in schools is that, while *time is a constant,* the curriculum is considered *variable* (i.e., expansive and flexible).

U.S. curriculum practice has been replete with numerous "add-ons" throughout its history (Kliebard, 1985, pp. 31-44). The practice continues into modern times with calls for such things as "global education," "education about AIDS," "student wellness," and many more. Such "add-ons" are rarely calculated in terms of their impact on other things in the curriculum as the convenient assumption is made that *somehow everything will fit!* Asking classroom teachers whether or not that assumption is true often can be a rude awakening to central office curriculum supervisors.

As a kind of work plan, curriculum should "fit" the time available for teachers to teach it. One of the reasons for the pervasive cynicism among teachers as to the real worth of curriculum guides is that they are not a "help" but "more work"; that is, they make the teachers' jobs more difficult, not easier. The attitude of cynicism is the result of decades of production of voluminous often vapid and tedious tomes that are not "user friendly" and do not assist teachers in setting priorities within the actual time constraints of the day.

Most often, curriculum guides assume there is more time to teach than is actually present because they do not account for the numerous and unplanned interruptions teachers face, the necessity to collect and distribute things to children, from lunch tickets to advertisements from booster groups, to take roll, and a host of other noninstructional chores that consume time allotted to teaching the content contained in the official curriculum guides of the district or school. Much of classroom teacher time is devoted to mechanical tasks imposed by the system that bear little relation to improving classroom instruction.

Too often, curriculum guides assume teachers possess a form of control that simply does not exist. For example, the impact of "pull-outs" at the elementary level severely hampers the capability of teaching the required curriculum with some of the students absent.

2.8 Setting Content Priorities and Expressing Time Values

Establishing time values within a curriculum and resolving the matter of how to get everything in that is deemed to be of "high" value requires the setting of priorities. Priorities can be established *before* a curriculum is written in the form of an ideology, or they can be developed *after* curriculum is written. There are strengths and weaknesses in either approach.

Setting the curriculum to a stated ideology ensures that the curriculum "fits" the ideology. Because much of what constitutes an ideology is "hidden," or implicit, however, the *before* model may be naive. It allows those hidden values and assumptions to remain unexpressed but dominant in the process. For example, to indicate that all children will pass a math test for demonstrated proficiency at a given level means that the statement accepts the content of the math test as appropriate, the values expressed in the content of the math questions as legitimate, and the role of the school in "teaching" that curriculum as viable. These are passed on without question in drafting a curriculum to meet this statement or standard.

All of these assumptions remain hidden or largely unexamined because they are accepted without question. In "front-end" curriculum work—the traditional approach in which philosophy-ideology is written first as a kind of preamble—the major weakness is that it reinforces the status quo because it fails to examine it at all. And the process tends to select means (curriculum) to match unexamined ends (assumed content and its values).

If the ideology or philosophy is written after the development of curriculum outcomes or indicators, then the creation or development of it can be deeply probed to reveal what the "real" values may be compared with the desired outcomes. This makes the development of the so-called rationale for curriculum much more public.

For example, after writing a curriculum indicator as "the desire to obtain a given score on a state math test," the question can be asked, "What are we really saying or meaning when this test and its content *become* our curriculum?" What are the implicit values and assumptions that *lie behind* this process? What is included on the test? What has been excluded from the test?

The approach of identifying the ideology *after* the curriculum outcomes are developed can be a useful but still flawed approach for setting priorities and the content of the curriculum. The flaw is that, without thinking about the values and assumptions *before writing* the curriculum, the indicators or outcome statements developed will contain value judgments that become self-reinforcing if an ideology is written that "reflects" the hidden biases of the outcome indicators.

Whatever values are contained in the outcome indicators, in turn, become the umbrella ideology. The question could be asked, "Where in this cycle are the excluded values and assumptions not part of the indicators considered?" If probing questions are not asked at all, it matters little whether the development of the real ideology happens first before curriculum is written or in the middle after indicators are developed.

Curriculum is always a means to somebody's end. The end is the state's, the school system's, the teacher's, or the board's. Somebody has a vested interest in whatever outcomes or content are designated. This means that behind every curriculum is a set of power relationships that are reinforced or not reinforced by any given curriculum.

From this perspective, no selection of curriculum content ever can be considered a politically neutral act. The selection of curriculum content is always a political process because it involves the designation of a body of knowledge that reinforces the existing or changing set of power relationships in the school or the larger society (see Schubert, 1986, pp. 140-160).

Various constituencies have a vested interest in the maintenance of any given set of power relationships. Those in power are loath to relinquish it or to countenance any activity or process that would seriously disturb or diminish it.

Asking questions, for example, about which groups or people have the most to gain or lose in society with the maintenance or change in any given curriculum means that one is probing for the linkages between the perpetuation of some knowledge at the expense of other types of knowledge. It is also illustrative of how curriculum development is intimately a political activity interlinked with an educational one. This is why such writings as Hirsch's (1988) *Cultural Literacy* are a hoax if passed off as a politically neutral (unbiased) activity. All knowledge benefits somebody and places someone else at a disadvantage.

To arrive at a system of priorities in selecting content, a simple sorting procedure can be used to eliminate much time-consuming discussion at the front end of curriculum development.

Teachers are asked, "What skills, knowledge, processes, attitudes, or [whatever content] should students possess after they leave Chemistry I, U.S. History, fifth grade math, or home economics?" Each topic or outcome is placed on a 3 × 5 index card, with one topic per card. At this point, the topics do not have to be developed into so-called behavioral objectives.

After each teacher has completed a set of cards, a general meeting is held to sort them. The first teacher might lead off by saying, "A concept that is most important in history is the role of geography in shaping people's attitudes and culture." Suppose that, of five teachers, all five agreed. All of the cards are grouped into one stack with a numerical value of five. The teacher continues with the others placing their cards in piles of fives, fours, threes, twos, and, if only one teacher has a concept, process, fact, or the like, then it is a singleton or one.

When the first teacher is out of cards, then the next teacher calls out his or her remaining cards and they are sorted into fours, threes, twos, and singletons. This continues until all teachers are out of cards.

At this point, the piles (fives, fours, threes, twos, and ones) are simply typed up and returned to the faculty. Because it is the "fives" that all teachers have included, this represents the "consensus" curriculum. There should be a discussion, however, about what didn't make it to the list of "fives." Teachers may wish to argue for the inclusion or exclusion of topics or objectives about which they feel strongly. In this discussion, the real consensus is hammered out. Topics that finally are included on the "fives" are candidates for inclusion in the curriculum to be developed.

One early way to determine whether the "fives" fit the available time is to perform a rough time approximation check. The procedure works this way.

Potential curriculum topics are placed in priority order (again by consensus), from first to last. Then the teachers estimate the amount of time it would take to successfully teach their children so that 90% or more actually learned the topic, objective, process, or fact. The time estimates are cast as the *least amount of time* to the *most amount of time*. An example is shown in Table 2.3.

In this example, time is expressed in ranges instead of as fixed points. The ranges have been established by the faculty based on their experience in teaching the topics with the students in the school(s) in which they work. A range of 1.5 to 3.0 means that, based on the teachers' actual experience, they have been able to reach mastery for 90% of their students in between 1.5 to 3.0 instructional periods.

When the "least amount of time" column is summed, the total number of class periods should not exceed the total possible in a quarter, semester, or year (whatever the official length of time is for the class) or *there is too much curriculum for the real time available.*

The least amount of time column represents an *ideal,* that is, *when everything goes right!* Because this does not occur very often, the actual amount of time is going to be more than was estimated. The "most amount of time" column essentially should be seen in terms of Murphy's Law; that is, given the likelihood that everything could go wrong, it does! In these cases, the time expressed will be more toward the maximum. But the designation of the time ranges means that at least 90% of the students can (and have) attained mastery in some time between these two numerical expressions.

The purpose of establishing the time ranges is to force the curriculum developers to confront the actual time issue teachers really face when trying to implement a curriculum with real

TABLE 2.3 Establishing Time Ranges for Topics in Instructional Periods for Physical Geography

Potential Priority Topics	Least Amount of Time	Most Amount of Time
1. Earth, sun, and moon	1.5	3.0
2. The plan of the Earth	1.0	3.0
3. World economy	3.0	7.0
4. The land	2.0	4.0
5. Gradation of running water	1.5	4.5
6. Economic relations of streams	1.0	5.5
7. Gradation by ice	3.5	4.5
8. Standing water	3.0	4.0
9. Gradation by ground water and wind	and so on	and so on
10. Soils		
11. The sea		
12. Coasts and ports		
13. The atmosphere		
14. Moisture in the air		
15. Climate		
16. Plant region		
17. Geography of animals		
18. The human species		
Totals		

children. The figure takes into account learning pace and other physical conditions that may be present in the school units in which teachers actually work. The time ranges should not be used to evaluate teachers. That is one of the fears teachers have in placing any estimate of time in a curriculum work plan.

If the principal is going to come into a classroom and "dock" a teacher for taking more time than that expressed in the curriculum work plan, teachers rightly refuse to provide any estimate of the expected time it might take to effectively deliver any curriculum. Time ranges force curriculum developers to create work plans that can be taught in the real time and conditions confronting teachers in their classrooms and schools.

Time ranges force curriculum developers (who may be teachers) to develop work plans that are realistic. The practice of facing the time and content priority issue nearly always reduces the size of curriculum guides. It reduces the "wish list" curriculum to one that is "realistic" and most likely to become the *taught curriculum*.

2.9 A Word About Sequence and Stress

The reader can tell from the table on physical geography that the topics are listed in numerical order. This "order" constitutes the *sequence* established for teaching physical geography. The order established in most curriculum guides is largely arbitrary, that is, more a product of being "logical" as opposed to being inherently "psychological." Most curricular sequences have more to do with gauging what should be taught first for the desired outcomes to be reached that involve those things (or topics, content) to be used later or toward the end of teaching.

Tests also establish curricular sequence. Where tests are given, they establish points by which teachers and school systems work back to create a sequence of instruction that prepares students to take the test. A rationale for a test to be given usually involves the major decision-making points in the educational system and has little to do with learning theory or child development.

Curriculum sequence is most often the creature of some logical-developmental order created with an individual curriculum content area that makes sense to scholars and practitioners in that field. Few, if any, are theoretically *grounded* in proven psychology that can be translated to pedagogical principles. The state of the art in terms of learning is far from the precision required to enable that kind of translation.

Stress or emphasis in a curriculum pertains to the extent that the topic or content receives considered attention. It is assumed that more important topics receive more time within any curricular sequence than the less important ones. Time spent is an indication of importance as well as of complexity. It is possible that something may be maximally important but not very demanding to do. For example, learning to wear safety goggles in a shop class is vital but takes little time except for occasional reminders from the instructor to wear them.

Some things are presented again and again in a curriculum with increasing levels of complexity added. This is the concept of a *spiral* or expanding base within a curriculum. For example, primary students may learn the Pledge of Allegiance by rote. They are continually exposed to the ideas within the pledge so that at some point they come to understand the abstract idea contained in the phrase, "one nation indivisible," a concept few primary students grasp entirely until maturation and instruction come together to enable them to truly understand (see Hunkins, 1980, p. 234).

2.10 A Recommended Curriculum Guide Format

When constructing curricular work plans, "small is beautiful." In the past, educators have paid too little attention to simple things such as the ways curriculum could be presented to make it easy to reference, use, take home, and compare with lesson plans or state-produced testing materials.

The assumption in the past has been that the ubiquitous three-ring binder is the best way to package curriculum. That this may not be so may come as a surprise. Three-ring binders are often quite bulky and, if they become too large, discourage teachers from taking them home to use in laying out units and lessons. The hidden message with three-ring binders is that the curriculum won't be around long enough to "bind" anyway, so don't spend too much time with it because it will be changed.

Too often, curriculum supervisors view the matter as perpetually engaging in curriculum development. Teachers, however, see it differently. Teachers are very "present oriented" as opposed to supervisors and principals who are "future oriented" (Wolcott, 1977). This fundamental difference between teachers and their supervisors is no more apparent than in the construction of curriculum guides. Teachers want something that is immediate, practical, applied, and "hands on." Curriculum guides too often are ethereal, vague, general-purpose outlines that defy practicality. One result is that, when alone behind their classroom walls, teachers junk the curriculum guide and reach for their textbooks.

A dog-eared curriculum guide ought to be enshrined as a paragon of virtue because it would mean that such documents were useful and referenced a lot. The idea is to make it easy to get curriculum guides out of bottom drawers, closets, and stacks of other papers by making them compact and accessible.

Curriculum guides ought to recognize that the teacher is the only person who can tie together (tighten) the essential elements of internal system control or focus and that the teacher usually does that task alone and unsupervised. Few human organizations are so totally dependent upon a single person working in isolation from all others and without formal supervision to attain important work task flow connectivity.

A recommended curriculum guide format is shown in Table 2.4. It consists of a single sample page from a larger curricular document in any subject. It links the content to be taught to textbooks and other materials, contains important classroom cues (without getting into elaborate cookbook recipes), and links all of these facets to tests in use and sample test items to deal with all aspects of alignment. The time to be spent is stated in time ranges rather than as fixed points.

Curriculum guide formats can be horizontal or vertical, but they must contain the essential elements by which the total quality of the curriculum can be tightened if necessary by each

TABLE 2.4 A Sample Curriculum Guide Format That Maximizes Local Control of Textbooks and Tests

Content to Be Taught	Textbook(s): Reference by Page	Other Materials Referenced	Classroom Cues	Tests in Use	Sample Test Item(s)	Recommended Time Ranges
Content can be stated as topics, skills, processes, themes, facts, values, attitudes, knowledge. Does not have to be stated in behavioral terms.	All textbooks that may be used should be listed and keyed by page to the first column. When teachers "follow" the guide, they should be moving around the textbooks rather than letting them "dictate" content and sequence.	All other extant supplementary materials should be keyed to column 1 and their location should be stated: (s) = school based, and (crs) = central resource based.	Important cues should be stated here by which the curriculum can be connected to classroom procedures or any special approach required to teach successfully should be indicated.	This column should key each topic or objective to any text that will measure them. This is "content" alignment.	By showing actual text examples, "context" alignment information is provided. These data can also be connected to the "classroom cues" column.	Time ranges should be normed locally by experienced teachers and include the largest share of the population that is possible. Use periods or modules for secondary schools and minutes or hours for elementary schools.

NOTE: The size should be small and compact. Avoid making curriculum guides "cookbooks" of methods and recipes, which tends to greatly increase their size. Likewise, curriculum guides are not substitutes for the teacher's guide of a textbook series. Guides should tie together the written, taught, and tested curricula.

classroom teacher using it. This is the idea of "loose-tight" management developed by Peters and Waterman (1982) in their best-selling book. A successful organization is "tight" on focus and vision and "loose" on methods and means (the how to's). So curriculum guides bind the system together at the necessary junctures to obtain optimal results over time.

References

Allen, M. J., & Yen, W. M. (1979). *Introduction to measurement theory.* Monterey, CA: Brooks/Cole.

Apple, M. (1986). *Teachers & texts.* New York: Routledge & Kegan Paul.

Armstrong, R., Cornell, T. D., Kraner, R. E., & Roberson, E. W. (1970). *The development and evaluation of behavioral objectives.* Worthington, OH: C. A. Jones.

Beauchamp, G. A. (1975). *Curriculum theory.* Wilmette, IL: Kagg.

Bowles, S., & Gintis, H. (1976). *Schooling in capitalist America.* New York: Basic Books.

Cetron, M., & Gayle, M. (1991). *Educational renaissance.* New York: St. Martin's.

Ellis, A. K., Mackey, J. A., & Glenn, A. D. (1988). *The school curriculum.* Boston: Allyn & Bacon.

English, F. W. (1987). *Curriculum management for schools, colleges, business.* Springfield, IL: Charles C Thomas.

Gagne, R. M., & Briggs, L. J. (1979). *Principles of instructional design.* New York: Holt, Rinehart & Winston.

Glatthorn, A. A. (1987). *Curriculum leadership.* Glenview, IL: Scott, Foresman.

Hall, E. T. (1977). *Beyond culture.* Garden City, NY: Anchor.

Hirsch, E. D., Jr. (1988). *Cultural literacy.* New York: Vintage.

Hunkins, F. P. (1980). *Curriculum development.* Columbus, OH: Charles E. Merrill.

Katz, M. B. (1987). *Reconstructing American education.* Cambridge, MA: Harvard University Press.

Kaufman, R., & English, F. W. (1979). *Needs assessment: Concept and application.* Englewood Cliffs, NJ: Educational Technology.

Kaufman, R., & Herman, J. (1991). *Strategic planning in education.* Lancaster, PA: Technomic.

Kliebard, H. M. (1985). Three concerns of American curriculum thought. In A. Molnar (Ed.), *Current thought on curriculum* (pp. 31-44). Alexandria, VA: Association of Supervision and Curriculum Development.

Lincoln, Y. S., & Guba, E. G. (1985). *Naturalistic inquiry*. Beverly Hills, CA: Sage.

Mager, R. F. (1962). *Preparing objectives for programmed instruction*. San Francisco: Fearon.

McLaren, P. (1986). *Schooling as a ritual performance*. London: Routledge & Kegan Paul.

McNeil, J. D. (1977). *Curriculum*. Boston: Little, Brown.

Mirande, A., & Enriquez, E. (1979). *La Chicana*. Chicago: University of Chicago Press.

Mitchell, C., & Weiler, K. (1991). *Rewriting literacy*. South Hadley, MA: Bergin & Garvey.

Montejano, D. (1987). *Anglos and Mexicans*. Austin: University of Texas Press.

O'Neill, W. F. (1981). *Educational ideologies*. Santa Monica, CA: Goodyear.

Payne, D. A. (1968). *The specification and measurement of learning outcomes*. Waltham, MA: Blaisdell.

Peters, T. J., & Waterman, R. H. (1982). *In search of excellence*. New York: Harper & Row.

Purpel, D. E. (1988). *The moral and spiritual crisis in education*. South Hadley, MA: Bergin & Garvey.

Schubert, W. H. (1986). *Curriculum*. New York: Macmillan.

Shor, I. (1986). *Culture wars*. Boston: Routledge & Kegan Paul.

Simon, R. I., Dippo, D., & Schenke, A. (1991). *Learning work*. South Hadley, MA: Bergin & Garvey.

Taba, H. (1962). *Curriculum development*. New York: Harcourt, Brace & World.

Wallace, D. G. (1981). *Developing basic skills programs in secondary schools*. Alexandria, VA: Association of Supervision and Curriculum Development.

Wolcott, H. F. (1977). *Teachers vs. technocrats*. Eugene, OR: Center for Policy and Management.

3

Aligning the Curriculum

Curriculum alignment refers to the "match" or overlap between the content and format of the test and the content and format of the curriculum (or curriculum surrogate such as the textbook). The closer the fit or match, the greater the potential improvement on the test. In essence, the learner must know both the content of the curriculum and how the test will be used to measure his or her knowledge or mastery of that content.

Curriculum alignment is a process to improve the match between the formal instruction that occurs in the school and the classroom and that which any test will measure. Figure 3.1 shows two ways curriculum alignment can be established.

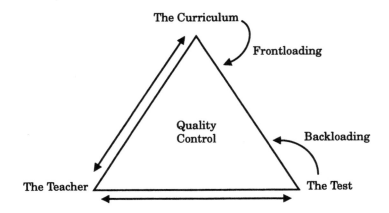

Figure 3.1. Curriculum Alignment: The Relationship Can Be Entered One of Two Ways

NOTE: Frontloading = establishing the "fit" by working from the curriculum to the test. Backloading = working from the test to the curriculum.

3.1 The Process of Alignment by Frontloading

The first way curriculum alignment can be established is through a process called *frontloading*. This practice means that the educator writes his or her curriculum first and then searches for an appropriate test to measure or assess whether or not students have learned that which the curriculum includes (see Lindvall & Nitko, 1975, pp. 12-26). Frontloading is nearly universal in being preferred as a practice in schools because it establishes the primacy of the curriculum to which the test must follow and not lead. In this scenario, the test always follows the curriculum and does not "establish" it.

This is a sensitive issue with local educators, who often fear that teaching to or from the test raises the issue of who possesses the expertise to establish any curriculum as well as its propriety. The assumption is that local educators know best, though that is often not the case.

Local educators are also acutely sensitive to the fact that tests, particularly standardized tests, may represent an extremely narrow and rigid view of the actual goals and objectives of any local curriculum. Teachers are extremely sensitive to this short-coming of standardized tests, with a good many believing that such tests are inappropriate measures of the learning process (see Smith, 1991).

A. *Problems With Frontloading*

Furthermore, locally developed tests are notoriously poor as instruments, lacking reliability and usually loaded on the bottom end of rote memorization test items requiring little, if any, upper-level thinking or problem-solving abilities on the part of the students. This situation often is reflective of the actual teaching situation, however, which is concentrated upon rote work in the great bulk of teaching time (see Lien, 1976, pp. 25-51).

In other cases, the local instructional program is far too complex and complicated to be used as the base to apply traditional standardized measures. A key example is that students in language experience or "whole language"-based programs, which are increasing in popularity, often fare poorly on traditional standardized tests of language acquisition, which are based on traditional reading approaches dominant in most reading textbooks. So one of the problems with frontloading as a practice is the lack of appropriate measures for determining success when the program is radically different than those upon which standardized tests are aligned.

B. *The Bogeyman of "Teaching to the Test"*

The practice of frontloading universally establishes that "teaching to the test" occurs. If a local educator writes a local curriculum, and then develops a local test to assess whether or not children have learned that local curriculum, when teachers teach *to* the local curriculum, they are also "teaching to the local test." If the curriculum and the test are virtually the same, *teaching to the test is inevitable and desired.* In fact, the extent to which any test is useful in reteaching any given curriculum is the extent to which that test does indeed measure the curriculum in the first place.

If the test provides data about some curriculum other than the one developed locally, the information may be interesting but it isn't useful in improving teaching or learning because it has little to do with what that teaching or learning is about, that is, as it pertains to the actual *content* of both processes. This is one reason that much of what data are produced by standardized tests aren't used at local levels. The fact is that the data have little do to with the actual curriculum in place at the local level.

c. *Critical Assumptions of Randomness Violated*

The makers of standardized tests desire a low alignment to any purely local curriculum (which means the test content doesn't match the local curriculum content directly). This has to be true or it would be possible for some districts to do much better than others simply based on the fact that some alignments were much better than others.

This situation would violate a critical assumption regarding randomness that all makers of standardized test instruments must assume. Randomness means that test scores can only be compared if all children who take the test have the same chance of learning that which it measures. Put another way: "This curve is often called a *normal* distribution curve because it approximates distribution according to the mathematical laws of probability or chance" (Lincoln, 1924, p. 33). If this were not so, some children would score better simply because of their circumstances, which in turn violates the principle of randomness or chance.

Early test makers assumed that it was possible to assess intelligence independently of the environment (Samuda, 1975, p. 63). This assumption is *false* because socioeconomic status does predict what a student's score will be on a standardized test, far more so than the school's curricula or its size (with an assumed low alignment to the local curriculum; see Fowler & Walberg, 1991).

This means that *wealth* predicts a student's score, and wealth is not a random variable in the larger society. Or, in the words of researcher Christopher Jencks (1972, p. 53), "Variations in what children learn in school depend largely on variations in what they bring to school, not on variations in what schools offer them." The fact that environmental factors such as socio-economic status and amount of schooling and language influenced test scores was postulated in 1935 by Klineberg.

Some psychometricians postulate that teaching anything about the test, its format, or content directly is an unethical practice (Haladyna, Nolen, & Haas, 1991). They posit that test items are drawn from a potential "bank" of items that are purported to assess a "construct of achievement." If one teaches to specific items, a pupil may look good but not actually understand the larger "construct" and so his or her score may be fallacious. The function of this argument is to deny to local educators any prior knowledge of what a test assesses, thus ensuring a random distribution of scores and a bell-shaped curve, the so-called normal distribution of scores.

This interstitial idea between what tests measure and the use of tests in making judgments about schools, teachers, and curricula is the logical link between the continued use of such tests and the capability of applying them to make judgments about the quality of that application locally. The so-called construct of achievement concept, if taken to the extreme advocated by some test purists, simply results in allowing race, sex, and wealth to predict test scores. Teachers are very aware of these shortcomings (Smith, 1991, p. 538).

D. *Textbooks as Curricula Affect Alignment and Test Scores*

Of course, local textbook adoption and the varying rates of alignment to known standardized tests shed new light on the impact of in-school factors. Leaving that fact aside for the moment, how then are such test data useful in improving the delivery of a purely local curriculum if they don't match that curriculum?

The answer is that low alignments to local curriculum cast serious doubts on the efficacy of standardized tests in really assessing what any local school or school system is attempting to do in the first place. The comparisons are not made to the local curriculum but to the place of other students who are also pursuing a vastly different curriculum or at least a curriculum whose similarity to any other local curriculum is unknown. Students can't be compared on content mastery because no claim can be made about content similarity from one site to the next or from one state to the next. All that can be said is that information from standardized tests shows how one student is doing compared with another student on an assumed or *mythical national curriculum* that is unspecified in the name of assessing the construct of achievement.

The great weakness of standardized tests in providing useful information to local classroom teachers and administrators is that the data they provide are practically of no use unless the alignment (match) with the local curriculum is known (see Resnick & Resnick, 1985, p. 12). When that becomes known, test data have a great deal of relevance to local educators and then become *feedback*. Feedback occurs when the data regarding the actual learning of students can be attached in concrete ways to what teachers are supposed to (and ultimately do) teach their students.

Frontloading as a practice preserves the idea of local control of the curriculum, although, with increasing reliance on standardized and statewide criterion-referenced tests (not to mention the historical reliance on textbooks, which have exercised a profound "standardizing impact" on the taught curriculum), such control is fast fading as a reality on the U.S. educational scene.

E. Disadvantages of Frontloading as a Curriculum Practice

The disadvantages of using frontloading as a dominant practice in the development of curriculum are that (a) no curriculum can ever be considered a purely localized product given the mobility of students and their families in the United States and (b) it takes an excessive amount of time to develop a curriculum *prior* to the time local educators may have the option of selecting a test that "matches" that local curriculum. As a by-product of the second problem, frontloading is the most expensive way to obtain alignment because an entire curriculum has to be written before it can be aligned.

F. *"Bubble-Up" Curriculum Practices in Schools*

Local curriculum practice in most school districts is dominated by a process that could be called "the bubble-up model of curriculum development." Essentially, this practice begins when groups of teacher are commissioned to "write" curriculum, usually in the summer. Such groups are rarely provided guidelines or formats or even information on basic concepts such as alignment or tightening.

What often emerges from such projects is a vague set of platitudes and cookbook-type lessons that are unrelated, that are incoherent in terms of overall focus, and that remain unevaluated or assessed.

"Bubble-up" curriculum models make a fuss about process but produce products that are unusable even by those who created them in the first place. Often, they are so ambiguous that test alignment is nearly impossible to attain because test item content is much more specific, and hence dominates the alignment process, and by default becomes a form of *backloading* instead of frontloading.

Although nearly all curriculum textbooks at the university level advocate a form of frontloading, when found in local school districts, the process is so undefined and open ended that the work plans produced by it are rarely "user friendly" and have little impact on what teachers do in actual classrooms when supervisors or administrators are not around. The primary weaknesses of frontloading are that it is expensive and unproductive. Teachers are reluctant to write very specific plans for fear that, as work-related documents, they may in turn be evaluated by the system officials using them. Such work documents are kept quite general and open ended to protect teachers against this form of work control.

The real agenda in *frontloading curriculum* revolves around defining the work to be done without also providing the means to enable closer supervision and evaluation from occurring simultaneously (see Dreeben, 1973). These two forces are contradictory and produce a tension that is usually never addressed and is left unresolved in local curriculum development.

G. *When Frontloading Is Impossible*

As a practice, frontloading is impossible whenever local educators must use a test with an unknown match to its local curriculum. Frontloading only works when local educators design their own curriculum and select their own test. If this is not possible, frontloading is not possible. The only real decision to be made is whether to backload or not.

3.2 The Process of Alignment via Backloading

Alignment refers to the "match" between the curriculum content to be taught and the test content to be used in assessing pupil learning. *Backloading* refers to the practice of establishing the match by working from the test "back to" the curriculum. It means that the test *becomes the curriculum*. In this case, there is always 100% alignment because the curriculum to be taught was derived from the test to be given.

A. *Implications of Backloading as a Practice*

There are two implications for this practice. The first is that whoever wrote the test also wrote the curriculum and, unless the test constructors were also local, local control is thus sacrificed. The second is that the issue of "teaching to the test" is raised as a possible source of unethical or unwise procedure.

The first issue of "local control" has already been addressed. One way to assess what may be lost by backloading is to examine the test itself (if possible) and determine whether there is anything on the instrument one believes ought not to be taught to students and thus tested. If the answer is negative, it matters little what the test is assessing because learners would have been taught what is present regardless.

Another check is more profound. A local educator may ask, "Is there anything that a local student should know that this test isn't assessing?" To answer that question, some frontloading has to occur because it assumes that the content of the curriculum is in some way knowable or known. How else would the question be answered? A purely *backloaded* curriculum would not ask the question, which concerns the "null curriculum," that is, the content not included in a curriculum. The act of "nonselection" is value laden and, in this case, the values nonselected by the test makers represent an unknown element that may be at odds with local values.

B. *The Issue of "Teaching to the Test"*

The issue of "teaching to the test" remains one of the most troublesome problems in the whole alignment process. Some researchers have called the idea of *alignment*—that is, matching the test and curriculum content—"unethical" (see Haladyna et al., 1991, p. 4).

What is unethical about the practice is that test makers desired a kind of response called the "normal curve," a frequency distribution of scores that looks like the bell shape in Figure 3.2.

To derive this shape, several assumptions are made about the scores. The first is that the property or variable being assessed exists in the larger population more or less like height or weight (see Mehrens & Lehmann, 1987, p. 41). This is a very debatable assumption. Nonetheless, to attain the "normal curve" in assessing learner outcomes, further assumptions have to be made regarding whether or not all the children start at the same point and/or that factors outside purely "learning" are not at work skewing the "normal" curve positively or negatively.

It has been noted already that socioeconomic level definitely skews learner outcomes, which do not assume a normal curve if large populations of learners from lower socioeconomic groups

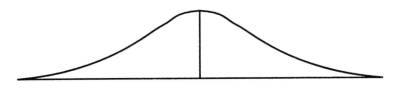

Figure 3.2. The Bell-Shaped Curve

NOTE: To arrive at a frequency distribution in the form of a bell-shaped curve, randomness or chance must be functional in order to get a continuous distribution of responses resembling this form. Yet, schools, teaching, administration, and curriculum cannot be considered "random" acts or "chance" variables. Test secrecy does not permit alignment and so school-related variables may appear random when they are not.

are included in a sample. So the act of comparison at the outset is specious unless the comparisons are explained.

For a normal curve to be desired as a frequency distribution, it has to be assumed that there is only a tangential relationship between the test and the curriculum (low alignment). If the alignment were not low, then those groups that engaged a curriculum with a higher match would do better on the test. If the alignment were quite high, there would be nothing wrong with teaching to the test because it wouldn't result in improved test scores.

Behind the quality of low alignment is the *assumption of randomness,* because whatever is being measured on a test is assumed to be *a continuous variable* (like height or weight). Anything else would not produce a normal distribution (see Popham, 1981, p. 159). If alignment occurs, then some persons or groups would score better than they would have had they not had access to this "match." The score distribution then becomes discontinuous or nonrandom as a result, producing a skewed or irregular distribution.

Another word for *random* is *chance.* Chance is the *critical* assumption that is absolutely essential in test theory (see Magnusson, 1966, pp. 4-8). It means that, if groups of students are going to be compared on some similar and assumed continuous variable, all should have not only the same opportunity to be selected in the sample but the same exposure to the variable being assessed and, furthermore, all should respond in the same fashion (see Bertrand & Cebula, 1980, p. 116).

If this were not so, some members would skew the distribution or frequency of scores whatever way their exposure matched or did not match the assessment tool or process. External factors to the school already skew student response on tests, which results in a noncontinuous distribution or nonrandom distribution.

Another problem lies in using test scores to compare students, teachers, administrators, and curriculum/programs, one to the other, based on such data. For such comparisons to be valid, one or more assumptions have to be made. All of them are specious (see Mehrens & Lehmann, 1968, p. 194).

The first assumption that has to be made is that the "treatments" received by the students in the first place were themselves continuous or random; that is, they assumed the properties of a normal distribution. This must be so for comparisons between students, and by inference then to teachers, administrators, and curriculum/programs, cannot be made. School itself has to be considered a random variable to result in the distribution of scores based on the idea of a continuous variable.

Yet, in reality, no school is a random variable. All schools are nonrandom, that is, *purposive places* where activities are goal directed. Administrators, teachers, and curricula are nonrandom variables as well. If judgments are going to be made about the quality or effectiveness of teachers, administrators, curricula, or programs on the basis of a test score, then it has to be conceded that they are *purposive variables and nonrandom by design* or schools cannot be accountable for what they do.

It has to be assumed that, if schools did something differently than they were doing before (a nonrandom act), then their actions would not result in the production of a continuous variable and a normal curve. A normal curve assumes that 50% of the population must be *below average* for the assumption regarding a continuous variable to hold.

Inasmuch as test scores are driven largely by socioeconomic factors, then schools that serve large populations of lower-socioeconomic students are automatically assigned to the "below average" category. This is *social determinism* based on wealth. It

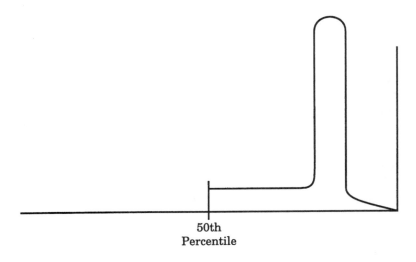

50th
Percentile

Figure 3.3. The "J" Curve
NOTE: The "J" occurs when all children are learning and "above average." Curriculum-test alignment at both the content and the context
levels is one way to approach the "J" curve.

doesn't matter what teachers or administrators do in developing
a curriculum or reforming programs, they will automatically be
"worse" based on the students they serve. In the words of one
Ohio legislator who viewed the test results of the first statewide
exam, "We spent a million and a half dollars to find out that poor
kids did worse than rich ones." The achievement test results
closely match socioeconomic level in most states and regions
around the United States (see Sax, 1980, pp. 373-379).

"Teaching to the test" is an issue with the test makers because
it tampers with the idea of test results being considered a continuous variable. If some students are taught what they are
tested on, they will obviously do better than if they were not so
instructed. Thus what is assumed to be a continuous variable
becomes skewed or discontinuous. Teaching to the test jams the
bell-shaped curve! It produces a "J" curve, which means that the
scores are all above average. The distribution is positively
skewed, as shown in Figure 3.3.

The classic problem in teaching to the test is that students are learning only the test item and not the concept, process, or idea that lies behind it (Cronbach, 1963, p. 681). So, if they score well on a test, the scores don't necessarily represent what they really know or don't know. Teaching to the test is therefore viewed by some as a kind of "pollution" of the "true meaning" of what a score might indicate if this condition were not present.

The major problem with this assertion is that test scores must assume the property of a continuous variable producing a bell curve to be considered rigorous, and alignment produces a nonrandom distribution of scores.

The most common form of a nonrandom test response occurs on the weekly spelling test so pervasive in the nation's elementary school classrooms. That procedure begins with the teacher introducing 25 words on Monday, the class studying those words through Wednesday, when a practice test is provided on the same 25 words, followed on Friday by a test that again measures the same 25 words. The classroom teacher does not sample these words. He or she does not resort to "Form B" of a test so that the words are unfamiliar to the students.

What is desired is a nonrandom response on the part of the class. Most teachers hope that all students will earn 100% and spell the 25 words!

If the teacher wanted a random distribution, he or she would not have taught the students at all about the 25 words. If one desires 50% of the class to be below average, the best way to ensure that this is the result is to avoid teaching students that which you intend to test them on because *teaching will make such a difference.*

Teaching will produce a nonrandom or nonnormal distribution, particularly if it matches the test. If one is not teaching what one is testing, how can judgments be made about the quality of teaching based on a test score? If a test does not match a school's curriculum, how can test scores be used as a measure of the quality of the curriculum?

Because tests do measure acquired behavior and learning, if that learning has not been acquired in school, it has to have been acquired somewhere. The answer is that it is acquired in the larger socioeconomic arena, which is why socioeconomic level plays such a large role in predicting test results. Students taking tests with low alignments are largely bounded by the lessons learned (or not learned) in their socioeconomic level.

Socioeconomic determinism is the consequence of using standardized norm-referenced tests, which pretend to be "objective" measures of pupil learning when they are anything but "objective." If such tests were truly objective, there would be no predictor variables that could account for their frequency except truly random cases. Wealth is not the same property as height and weight. And in no case should school or school-related factors such as teaching, administration, or curriculum development be considered random variables.

But a test with a low alignment to a school's teaching or curriculum makes it appear as if factors were random because none of them predicts the scores (because there is scant or no connection between what is going on in classrooms and the extent to which any kind of measurement is aligned). Low test-curriculum alignment makes it appear as if schooling were a continuous, random variable. If schooling truly were such a random variable, then all of the purposive activities in a school that direct and focus teaching would be fixed ahead of time by the communities in which they happen to be located and their socioeconomic conditions.

If, then, tests are to be used to assess pupil learning, quality teaching, sound administration, and productive curriculum, they have to have a planned overlap to what these activities are about. When that overlap is planned so that what one measures is what one wants to occur, *alignment is present and the measurement does not produce a normal curve*. The frequency distribution will resemble a much more positively skewed result than the bell-shaped template so familiar in testing circles.

Comparison of students, teachers, administrators, curricula, programs, and the like must be made on the basis of a test tightly aligned to their activities or (a) the scores cannot be considered valid indicators of the activities and (b) scores cannot be compared validly in terms of doing anything about them to improve subsequent outcomes.

The major problem with the bell curve is that it is precisely the wrong distribution of scores to assess *purposive behavior that is essentially nonrandom by design, which is the essence of schooling!* Ralph Tyler (1974) noted that achievement testing in World War I was strongly linked to intelligence testing, which assumed a normal curve. Says Tyler (1974, p. 147), "Actually, school programs are based on contrary assumptions." Continuous warnings against "teaching to the test" allow nonschool variables to dominate and predict test scores rather than in-school variables predicting them. It dooms schools and school systems serving lower socioeconomic children always to being labeled "poor schools" when what they should properly be labeled is "schools serving the poor." The answer is that schools should test what they teach and teach what they test.

C. Dealing With Unethical Applications of Standardized Tests

To be used properly, standardized tests assume that all in-school variables can be factored in such a way that they can be "random" and, if influential, take on the characteristics of a continuous variable. If this were not so, the bell-shaped curve could not be considered the proper "form" in displaying the scores obtained on the test norms. To control for possible bias in the sample of respondents constituting the norm, great care has to be taken in selecting those included. If mostly Quakers were somehow part of a test group and a question about war were asked, the preponderance of pacifists would provide a very different distribution than one in which Quakers were not a majority.

If all of the school districts in a state that intended to use some sort of state standardized test were assessed on an assumed random variable, the distribution of scores would be expected to resemble a bell curve. By definition, on any characteristic, 50% of the school districts are expected to be "below average." If a state makes no move to punish those school districts on the bottom (who are more than likely to be poor in terms of extant socioeconomic variables), then the test simply reflects the bias in the various communities in which the schools function. "Teaching to the test" may change the distribution but, if no judgments are being made about the quality of teaching, curriculum, administration, and the like, it doesn't really matter what the score is.

If the state, its agents, or other public persons are going to punish the school district, its schools, teachers, or administrators based on a test score, however, then the results of the test have been unethically applied (see Cangelosi, 1991, p. 105).

First, the bell-shaped curve *requires* a 50% failure rate, and no distribution would be accepted as accurate unless this were the case. Second, teaching, curriculum development, and administration are not random acts but purposive, goal-directed ones. Change the goal of teaching to include more of the content of the test and the scores will improve on the same test. Tests cannot be used to assess these characteristics if they don't match up with what is being taught. The whole assumption of purposiveness requires alignment to be present. Otherwise, the data are useless in terms of trying to improve because there is no fit to what is being assessed. Furthermore, if teachers, students, and administrators can't improve with subsequent tests, how can the data be used to measure their effectiveness? In other words, if test data acquisition has no "effects," what is the value of having the test in the first place?

It is unethical to "teach to a test" if the purpose of the test is truly to assess a random variable that is assumed to contain the characteristics of a continuous variable within the population being assessed. In this scenario, it would imprudent to make judgments that at the base *assume* that characteristics indirectly connected to the variable (quality of teaching, administration, curriculum development) being directly assessed (for example, a student achievement score in math) are essentially continuous as well.

Once such an indirect variable is affected by changes derived from a test score, it ceases to be random even if it were so considered initially. Thus the logic of standardized tests breaks down when moving from direct assessment of the assumed psychological properties of students (learning) to those factors that are supposed to be important in producing the effects but that are noncontinuous and nonrandom in nature. Sooner or later, those indirect factors cease to be random.

That has to be the case if such variables are to be judged in some way as to effectiveness or performance. One cannot continually blame teachers for poor test scores if their behavior has no impact on learning. So teaching has to be envisioned as a purposive, nonrandom, noncontinuous activity that does not assume the properties of a bell-shaped curve (see Smith, 1991).

The norm of assessment in most other human activities, from manufacturing to athletics, is that one always teaches to the test. The basketball coach would never be told by the principal, "Your team may not practice, that would be cheating! Furthermore, you may not scout the other team or obtain films of the other team. You may not know what offense or defense they plan to run at your team. That would all be cheating! Just get your team ready to play by telling them, 'Don't think about the game at all. When the time comes, just do the best you can!'"

No basketball coach would accept these conditions in a competitive basketball league. But we tell classroom teachers virtually the same thing all the time when it comes to "practicing for the achievement test."

No manufacturer would use an assessment instrument to measure worker performance that wasn't indexed to the product being turned out and its quality. Worker performance is only relative to the product and its quality. And no manufacturer wants a bell curve! That would mean 50% of the products would be rejects. So the assessment of manufacturing goods is indexed (aligned) to the product being produced. Worker performance is directly keyed to the product. Measurement criteria are indexed to the product so that they match. Otherwise, using "feedback" would not be very useful in improving the product with subsequent applications in production.

It is this fact that lies at the heart of the statement that the bell-shaped curve is an inappropriate distribution to assess the quality of schools, the teaching in them, or the quality of the curriculum being used by teachers in their work. So what is unethical behavior?

If, on the other hand, the curriculum and the test are matched (aligned), and everyone knows what the alignment is, then the quality of teaching, of curriculum, and of administration can be assessed, and directly, because the fact of "no surprises" for the students has been ruled out as a *causative factor* in explaining the differences between the scores. The determinism of socio-economic level is decreased as a predictor. The school now becomes *the* qualitative factor in explaining pupil achievement because achievement scores are directly related to what happens in them.

In sports, if every team scouts every other team, practices against their preferred offense and defense, then the quality of their preparation and practice, their motivation and conditioning, become the determiners of the results. It is highly unlikely that these characteristics assume the form of a bell-shaped curve. They are much more likely to be a "J" curve, clustered near the positive end of the curve producing a tight skew. "J" curves have been called by Allport (1932, as cited in Guilford, 1936) measures of "institutional behavior."

Local educators in some states are continually confronted with a scenario in which the state education agency is going to test all the children in the state but actually desires a 50% failure rate embodied in a bell curve. The only way that such a distribution can occur is to keep the test a secret, which ensures randomness because it means that the content, the format, and the procedures contained in the test are unknown to everyone.

In this procedure, the purposiveness (nonrandomness) of the school has been negated by excluding the test content from the curriculum and from the teaching practices. The school therefore can be statistically treated as a random variable producing a continuous variable. However debatable this procedure may be, logically no judgments can be made about the quality of schools because those variables that are purposive (teaching, curriculum, grouping, and so on) have been reduced to random (nonpurposiveness) variables by keeping the test a secret and ensuring a low alignment of the test content with the curriculum content.

In such a scenario, the impact of the curriculum is negligible. This was demonstrated by the Coleman study of 1966 in which standardized achievement tests were used to probe for school-related variables that would have an effect upon pupil achievement. That study noted that "differences between schools account for only a small fraction of differences in pupil achievement" (Coleman, 1966, p. 22). The assumption upon which such differences rest is that "schools are remarkable similar in the way they relate to the achievement of their pupils" (p. 21).

What has happened here is that, by forcing a low content-content alignment from test to curriculum, in-school variables that could make a difference are blunted and don't make a difference. This undergirds the argument that schools are random (or all alike), in which case they become random by using random inclusion procedures. The result is a bell-shaped curve when pupil characteristics—their race and socioeconomic status—form the base for the distribution of scores as opposed to any in-school purposive (nonrandom) variable such as curriculum or facilities.

D. *What Is Cheating on Tests?*

Psychometric purists would define *cheating* as teaching anything remotely concerned with a test. It has been shown that their loyalty is given to assumptions regarding randomness and the necessity to base their predictions on a normal curve of the distribution of scores centered on ideas behind intelligence testing (see Jensen, 1980, pp. 71-74). Intelligence is assumed to be a characteristic like height or weight in the overall population and was named "general intelligence" so that tests could assess it similarly (see Terman, 1916, pp. 36-50). Results from using the Binet test in America were assumed to be biological rather than cultural even though Binet himself did not envision intelligence as biological (see Marks, 1981, pp. 18-19). Any "tampering" with test items believed to be biological (as opposed to cultural) that would not result in obtaining a normal distribution would be considered a violation of some underlying (and hence "true") "natural" condition.

That this is *the assumption* is shown by the analogy of some psychometricians to teaching someone to read a Snellen eye chart and then, when attaining a better score, attributing the gain to "better" eyes (Mehrens & Kaminski, 1988). If one expects to find a normal distribution based on biology, then any attempt to alter that distribution would be prohibited. Psychometricians who believe in "biological determinism" call any such intrusions "pollution" or "unethical practices."

As we have seen, however, there is a considerable body of professional opinion that the bell curve is inappropriate in assessing pupil achievement related to classroom teaching and purposive (nonrandom) behavior patterns. Philip Morrison (1977, p. 89), a physics professor at the Massachusetts Institute of Technology, has written, "I am disturbed that the sophisticates of educational statistics have written so little about the other distributions [those other than the bell-shaped curve] . . . Until they have done so, I rest fearful that they have mistaken mere consistency for observation, and a circle for a clear line of argument." What Morrison means is that the results of such tests should not be used to rate teachers, schools, or curricula because these factors are not distributed randomly in the population to be sampled, even though statistical assumptions and attendant secrecy result in reinforcing the belief that they are random and nonpurposive.

In reality, schools, teachers, and curricula cannot be random variables assuming the dimensions of a bell or Gaussian (for the mathematician Karl Gauss) curve. If they were, the whole idea of *accountability* would be absurd, and the purpose of such tests is to *establish accountability*. This basic logical incompatibility between biologically determined test norms and engaging in judgments about the quality of schools, teachers, principals, and curricula has led some to call for a moratorium on all standardized testing (Fine, 1975, p. 140).

Cheating on tests may be construed as allowing students to see or practice with the actual test itself prior to its administration,

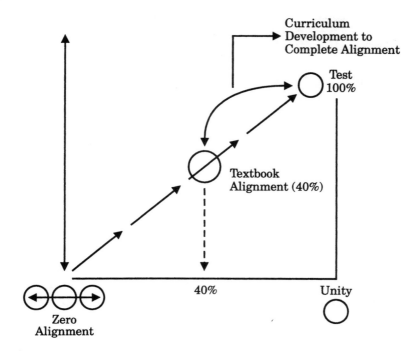

Figure 3.4. Preliminary Alignment Practices
NOTE: This is a display of a "backload" using textbook adoption to test as a measure of alignment. Curriculum development then is employed to complete the alignment.

providing students with more time than is allotted to complete their answers, assisting students to solve test items during the test, or changing student answers after the test has been taken.

3.3 How to Do Alignment

We have now seen how alignment can work from a frontloading perspective or from the view of backloading. The most common form of frontloading occurs in the textbook adoption cycle. If alignment is part of the criteria by which textbooks as work plans are adopted, then the books with the highest alignment should be adopted. Figure 3.4 shows this process.

Figure 3.4 shows the adoption of a textbook based on the test (a backload). In frontloading, the textbook with the maximum match to the local curricular outcomes would be adopted. Suppose that a text is adopted that produces a 40% match to the local curricular outcomes. Then local curriculum development would be required to complete the remaining 60%. The same figures would hold on a backload if the test is what is being matched to the textbook.

A. Determine the Context in Which Alignment Will Occur

How a school or school district approaches the alignment issue must be largely determined by the context in which the process is to occur. Propriety of alignment, and whether one should *frontload* or *backload*, is set by the contextual scenario surrounding the alignment issue.

If a school or school system is facing an externally imposed testing program in which the test makers desire a bell-shaped curve (a 50% failure rate), and negative consequences accrue to the school or the school system after the test has been administered, then the situation is one in which local officials should seriously consider backloading. This may be difficult given the climate of secrecy that often prevails when states or other external agencies desire to assess schools or school districts on test items that, if exposed publicly, would allow learning to occur, thus skewing the results more positively than is desired. (It may be observed that nothing messes up a bell curve more than pupil learning!)

School district teachers and officials have to watch carefully that their actions are not labeled "teaching to the test" when they take steps to backload. The "ethics" of testing often prohibit backloading in any form except a very general one, and context alignment is usually forbidden.

There are at least two levels of alignment. The first is *content alignment* in which the content of the test is matched to the content of the curriculum. The second level is *context alignment*, sometimes called *format alignment,* in which the shape of the assessment item is taught as well as the content of the item.

Thus, if spelling is to be tested, the way it is tested is as important as the words to be assessed. Typically, standardized tests use a form of word recognition as the method for assessing spelling. Spelling, however, is usually taught as direct recall of the way a word is derived from sounds provided orally by the teacher. One may be able to recognize a correct word when given but be unable to reproduce it from scratch when oral cues alone are provided.

Makers of standardized tests sometimes balk at providing format examples of test items, even though, with such nationally standardized tests as the Graduate Record Exam, examples may be purchased in book form prior to taking the test. Format or context alignment is an important variable in any testing scenario. Providing information about format is helpful in preparing students to take tests. If this were not so, most graduate students would not be asking their instructors if the final exam will be true/false, multiple choice, or essay in nature.

Any athletic coach will want to know what offense or defense an opponent will run so as to prepare his or her team to recognize these forms and respond accordingly. In football, the whole concept of "audibles"—that is, changes of play calling at the line of scrimmage—is based on the recognition of the "format" facing the offensive team.

Alignment is a very old concept in education. Much of the theory behind it was developed by Thorndike (1913) in his creation of the "identical theory of the transfer of training" and later expanded to the transfer by *generalization.* What this idea means is that, "unless the new situation has enough in common with the previous one for the learner to perceive applications, no transfer occurs" (Klausmeier & Goodwin, 1966, p. 473).

Alignment is facilitated when situations are taught so that the learner more readily recognizes them when they occur. It would be like a quarterback learning to read the defenses of the opponent quickly enough to call audibles. The quarterback must be able to "transfer" the knowledge of which play works best against which defense by moving from one situation (a play called in anticipation of a set defense) to a different play (when the situation encountered was not the one anticipated). *Transfer* is facilitated when the situations are similar and recognizable by the learner. *Alignment* is a process of teaching the learner to recognize similar situations (content and formats) by which assessment will take place.

In situations where test results are very negatively applied, and poor scores trigger even more undesirable consequences like inspections, sanctions, or takeover possibilities, local school officials should consider backloading from tests to localized work plans that teachers follow in the form of simple checklists to teach specific content, examples of formats, or specially developed curricula that include both.

Care must be taken so as to operate within state-defined limitations of test-curriculum matchups. If these are prohibitive, district or school officials may wish to take on officials or regulations that operate on the assumption that scores must follow the laws of "natural" determinism where results form a continuous variable in a bell-shaped curve. Officials may obtain data from the state showing that socioeconomic variables are the strongest predictors of pupil performance, and not school-related ones. The "biological" basis of the bell curve is much more culturally produced than the policymakers will find comfortable.

The "tightness" of the fit between backloading from the test, shaping teaching to ensure alignment, and curriculum construction is shaped by the requirements of the situation. "Tightening" occurs when the children involved are nearly dependent upon the school as the only avenue open to them to perform well on the tests. The schools cannot depend upon the socioeconomic level of their community to hold up their test scores because it is already quite low. The only means to improve a test score is to teach that which the test will measure and to do it well.

B. *Determine the Most Cost-Effective Form of Backloading*

The form backloading takes is contingent upon (a) how much time the school or system has to improve test scores, (b) the resources at the school or system's disposal, (c) the nature of the pupils and teachers involved, (d) the complexities of the test itself, and (e) the extent of the alignment extant in existing textbooks and other forms of school curricula in use.

If the school or the system has very little time in which to improve test scores before sanctions are applied, the creation of simple checklists geared to the test are probably the most efficacious form of backloading. The second step is to make sure teachers know how to perform the content and skills, procedures, and protocols required by the test so that their classroom teaching includes all of these areas. Staff development becomes a crucial ingredient of any successful backloading program.

It ought to be mentioned that the purchase of sophisticated hardware packages, learning laboratories, computers, and the like will not improve alignment unless it is specifically determined prior to any such purchase. There is nothing "magical" about hardware and labs unless the curriculum of the test and the content of the computers are aligned. Such materials are now no more aligned than the simple purchase of textbooks would ensure.

c. *After Backloading, Determine Results and Gains*

The efficacy of backloading is very limited and confined to the test itself. How much gain was recorded? Using the computer printouts from the test, perform an item analysis. Pinpoint where pupil responses were disappointing.

D. *Locate Curricular Breakdowns in Extant Work Plans*

To use test results to improve measured pupil performance, item analysis must be used to "link back" to whatever form of curriculum (or work plan) was being followed by classroom teachers. The "linking back" to the work plan is called "the reconnect." It means that test results are analyzed and reconnected or linked back to the work plans teachers were following. In this process, care is taken to ensure that changes are made in the work plans that will enhance measured pupil performance on future tests. This is the idea of *feedback*. An example would be a football team watching the films of the Saturday game on Monday to determine how best to improve their performance in subsequent practices and games. In fact, their gaps in performance *define the nature of practice*. The same idea would hold in the classroom.

E. Use Pareto Analysis to Correct the Important Errors

In analyzing mistakes, the Pareto Principle is usually followed; that is, the few account for the many (Burr, 1976, p. 203). The "few" in this case are deemed to be "fundamental errors," which will account for the greatest number of mistakes. This idea has been used with great effectiveness in the application of quality circles (Thompson, 1982, pp. 104-105) and is named after the great Italian economist and sociologist, Vilfredo Pareto (Powers, 1987).

In reviewing test scores and items, for example, suppose that two or three errors account for nearly 53% of all errors. With the correction of these two or three, 53% of all errors may be corrected in subsequent performances. Instead of trying to correct every error, the Pareto Principle gives educational leaders the opportunity to select those that affect that greatest number of pupils, thus improving the size of the group doing better on subsequent tests. In statistics, the "n," or size of the number of persons in the sample, is a significant factor in improving measures of central tendency, that is, mean scores or group averages.

The principal or teacher leader will examine test results and select those that the largest number of students missed, looking for common patterns that unite them together. Once identified, these are "reconnected" to the work plan or curriculum and a revised set of instructions is provided for teachers to follow.

F. Construct Revised Work Plans
Based on Pareto Analysis

This new set of directions based on Pareto analysis includes provisions for improved teaching of the tested concepts, skills, or content. Thus, by a continual iteration of working "back" from the test results, curriculum is more clearly focused on providing systematic instruction to pupils so that, with subsequent test iterations, their scores improve.

If the test is assessing complex problems that contain many skills, concepts, and knowledge, the "working back" to reconnect the test data to the curriculum (or textbooks) will stretch across more than one grade level. That means that the "correction" of the curriculum will involve multiple grades and more than one teacher over more than a year's period of time. Tracking back into a curriculum and redistributing the tested content may involve the development of "pacing charts." Such work plans involve the development of lessons over an extended time period that emphasize those areas in which alignment was poor or pupil performance was poor and concentrated teaching must occur in the designated areas. All tests are cumulative measures of pupil learning; that is, they assess not only what was taught at all grades before assessment but the "null" as well. The "null" represents what wasn't taught that should have been taught. Because tests are cumulative measures, where test scores indicate a problem is not necessarily where the problem is located or even corrected in the overall curriculum of a school or school system.

3.4 Other Issues in the Alignment Procedure

Backloading to obtain alignment can produce very quick results in improved test scores (see Niedermeyer & Yelon, 1981, pp. 618-620). Written, multiple choice tests, however, are an inappropriate tool to assess many areas of desired learning that a sound curriculum may include.

Using tests as the source to develop curriculum runs the risk of accepting and defining learning only in terms of what can be assessed on a paper and pencil test within a multiple choice format. The means to assessment, and its inherent limitations, become the ends themselves and place a cap on the possibility of learning outside that which tests are assessing. That would be a tragedy of enormous proportions.

Backloading should be considered an interim measure to improve test scores and not as any kind of final answer to determining what should be in a curriculum in the first place. Considering what children should know is the quintessential problem facing the schools. That always involves the frontloading approach, and it should remain dominant despite the presence of increasing "high-stakes" testing and all of the negative consequences that accrue to students, teachers, and parents with their continued use.

References

Bertrand, A., & Cebula, J. P. (1980). *Tests, measurement, and evaluation*. Reading, MA: Addison-Wesley.

Burr, I. W. (1976). *Statistical quality control methods*. New York: Marcel Dekker.

Cangelosi, J. S. (1991). *Evaluating classroom instruction*. New York: Longman.

Coleman, J. S. (1966). *Equality of educational opportunity*. Washington, DC: Government Printing Office.

Cronbach, L. J. (1963). Evaluation of course improvement. *Teachers College Record, 64*, 672-683.

Dreeben, R. (1973). The school as a workplace. In R. M. W. Travers (Ed.), *Second handbook of research on teaching* (pp. 450-473). Chicago: Rand McNally.

Fine, B. (1975). *The stranglehold of the I.Q.* Garden City, NY: Doubleday.

Fowler, W. J., Jr., & Walberg, H. J. (1991). School size, characteristics, and outcomes. *Educational Evaluation and Policy Analysis, 13*(2), 189-202.

Guilford, J. P. (1936). *Psychometric methods*. New York: McGraw-Hill.

Haladyna, T. M., Nolen, S. B., & Haas, N. S. (1991). Raising standardized achievement test scores and the origins of test score pollution. *Educational Researcher, 20*(5), 2-7.

Jencks, C. (1972). *Inequality*. New York: Basic Books.

Jensen, A. R. (1980). *Bias in mental testing*. New York: Free Press.

Klausmeier, H. J., & Goodwin, W. (1966). *Learning and human abilities*. New York: Harper & Row.

Klineberg, O. (1935). *Race differences*. New York: Harper.

Lien, A. J. (1976). *Measurement and evaluation of learning*. Dubuque, IA: William C. Brown.

Lincoln, E. A. (1924). *Beginnings in educational measurement.* Philadelphia: J. B. Lippincott.

Lindvall, C. M., & Nitko, A. J. (1975). *Measuring pupil achievement and aptitude.* New York: Harcourt Brace Jovanovich.

Magnusson, D. (1966). *Test theory.* Reading, MA: Addison-Wesley.

Marks, R. (1981). *The idea of IQ.* Washington, DC: University Press of America.

Mehrens, W. A., & Kaminski, J. (1988). *Using commercial test preparation materials for improving standardized test scores: Fruitful, fruitless, or fraudulent?* East Lansing: Michigan State University School of Education.

Mehrens, W. A., & Lehmann, I. J. (1968). *Standardized tests in education.* New York: Holt, Rinehart & Winston.

Mehrens, W. A., & Lehmann, I. J. (1987). *Using standardized tests in education.* New York: Longman.

Morrison, P. (1977). The bell shaped pitfall. In P. L. Houts (Ed.), *The myth of measurability.* New York: Hart.

Niedermeyer, F., & Yelon, S. (1981). Los Angeles aligns instruction with essential skills. *Educational Leadership, 38*(8), 618-620.

Popham, W. J. (1981). *Modern educational measurement.* Englewood Cliffs, NJ: Prentice-Hall.

Powers, C. H. (1987). *Vilfredo Pareto.* Newbury Park, CA: Sage.

Resnick, D. P., & Resnick, L. B. (1985). Standards, curriculum, and performance: A historical and comparative perspective. *Educational Researcher, 14*(4), 5-21.

Samuda, R. J. (1975). *Psychological testing of American minorities.* New York: Dodd, Mead.

Sax, G. (1980). *Principles of educational and psychological measurement and evaluation.* Belmont, CA: Wadsworth.

Smith, M. L. (1991). Meanings of test preparation. *American Educational Research Journal, 28*(3), 521-542.

Terman, L. M. (1916). *The measurement of intelligence.* Boston: Houghton Mifflin.

Thompson, P. C. (1982). *Quality circles.* New York: American Management Association.

Thorndike, E. L. (1913). *The psychology of learning: Vol. 2. Educational psychology.* New York: Teachers College, Bureau of Publications, Columbia University Press.

Tyler, R. (1974). The use of tests in measuring the effectiveness of educational programs, methods, and instructional materials. In R. W. Tyler & R. M. Wolf (Eds.), *Crucial issues in testing* (pp. 143-156). Berkeley, CA: McCutchan.

4

Auditing the Curriculum

4.1 The History and Development of the Curriculum Audit

The first curriculum audit was described in Leon Lessinger's famous, best-selling book, *Every Kid a Winner* (1970). In this prescient publication, Lessinger modeled a financial audit and indicated that, to reestablish public trust, school district officials should invite qualified auditors in to examine their records of performance against their own local objectives. These officials would then issue a public report, exactly like a financial audit. This process was called an "educational performance audit" (EPA). The first EPA was conducted in the Columbus Public Schools, in Ohio, in 1979.

92

From that date to the current time, more than 50 audits have been conducted in 25 states. Among them have been audits of school systems in both financial and instructional trouble and systems that have long-established records of excellence. Six audits have been used in federal or state courts or in litigation proceedings as data relevant to pupil performance, financial support, curriculum progress, facility adequacy, and school integration. The curriculum audit has established itself as a document of candor, rigor, and scope, one that communicates well with the lay public as well as with elected boards of education and education professionals.

4.2 External or Internal Audit?

The external curriculum audit has these advantages:

- No training of staff is required to conduct the audit, so start-up can be relatively quick.
- Public confidence in the findings and recommendations is enhanced when the audit is done externally.
- The external auditors serve as "lightning rods" for the inevitable "backlash" of certain groups within the staff whose interests have not been enhanced by the audit.
- If the "boss" is part of the problem, whether the superintendent or the board, he, she, or it will appear in the audit and be identified.
- External audits build political leverage for quick system changes that have a high acceptance rate among major constituencies because of the data base developed and because the audit is perceived as neutral by the major political stakeholders in the school system.
- External audits often can be funded by the business community or agency/foundation as a "one-of-a-kind" expense.

On the other hand, external audits are politically risky for tenured superintendents of long standing because of the inevitable "finger pointing" that may follow from various constituencies. They also carry the "risk" of not adhering to the system's public relations image it may feel it has worked hard to create. The sudden appearance of a document that "tells it like it is" may be detrimental to a carefully cultivated "always positive" story about the schools.

The advantages of an internal audit are these:

- The audit can be done in a leisurely fashion, with a schedule that is least disruptive to the operations of the school system.
- The political "risk" to the superintendent and the board is lessened rather considerably.
- Although staff have to be trained, the overall cost of the audit is usually substantially reduced.
- Partial audits can occur on selected aspects of the system over an extended time period of several years.
- After training, the "expertise" to conduct an audit is kept in-house and does not exit the system.
- If pursued over a number of years, internal auditing can become an accepted "way of life" in the system, improving its quality quietly and in an evolutionary manner.

The disadvantages of internal auditing are in public perception that those engaged in the audit are not without bias because they already work in the system and may have something to gain from their recommendations, and that the real "hard" findings and recommendations have been "sugarcoated" to make them palatable to insiders at the expense of a "rigorous" and objective examination. If internal staff are not trained well, an audit can be botched in its design and delivery and become a product of questionable quality. Finally, if the "real problem" is at the top of the organization, how many internal audits can really be candid about such dilemmas? This twist was noted by Aristotle in his book *Politics* when he said, "Most people are bad judges of their own interests" (Mansfield, 1989, p. 64).

Whether external or internal, these facts pertain to either approach in curriculum auditing:

- Auditors have to be trained to engage in the process.
- Audits take time.

- Audits cost money, whether to pay for the auditors outside the system or to take "in-kind" staff time of those already on the payroll.
- Audits contain some risk of a political nature to those in office; that is, there is no "fail-safe" process to review administrative decisions and their impact over time.

Whether internal or external, curriculum audits involve many other factors and conditions that should be examined prior to undertaking one.

4.3 The Necessary Conditions to Engage in Auditing

Several conditions are necessary to conduct any audit, whether it is of curriculum or the financial transactions of the system as contained in its official fiduciary documents. These conditions are as follows.

A. *The Existence of Standards*

When comparing actions, performance, or facts as contained in records, site visitations, or interviews, these data must be related to some sort of *expectations* in order to ascertain whether there are problems. In a financial document, such expectations are called *GAAP,* or Generally Accepted Accounting Principles.

GAAP represents a consensus by auditors on what to make of certain contingencies encountered in examining financial records. The consensus may relate to conventions, interpretations, or practices as to how an institution is supposed to represent its financial condition to the public and to its stockholders. Periodically, accountants and the courts add or change such conventions in GAAP.

GAAP provides the basis for a *discrepancy analysis* of financial records. Financial practices may be said to meet, exceed, or be below such standards. The basis for most kinds of evaluation does involve the establishment of standards or conventions. In education, both the tradition of accreditation and the reporting of statistical research studies use such bench marks (see Elashoff & Snow, 1971).

B. *The Existence of Data Trails and Records*

In addition to standards, any auditing procedure involves the review of data (Sayle, 1981). Such data represent proceedings, decisions, memorabilia, or consequences/outcomes of individuals or groups involved in the process being audited. When standards are present, data trails can be ascertained to lead to and support the activities of the organization being reviewed.

The existence of standards means those engaging in the external review can ascertain the extent to which the conclusions, outcomes, products, or consequences were or were not timely, accurate, of high quality, or justified.

If sufficient data are not present to support a judgment about whether or not the standard has been met, then no judgment is offered. Instead, the auditor "finds" that the organization cannot be judged because of the lack of sufficient evidence to do so. This is even more damaging in some cases than if the data were flawed. If an organization cannot be audited, then not only can the auditor not make any claims about its effectiveness but the organization itself lacks supporting data for claims it has developed. The *credibility* of the organization to its own publics is called into question.

C. *The Presence of Valid and Reliable Procedures*

Audits themselves involve procedures and assumptions that should be subject to scrutiny as well. The procedures used in an audit should relate to that which is being examined (a kind of "face" or content validity), and they should be consistently employed within the audit and in others conducted (a kind of reliability).

Audit validity involves developing a professional consensus about what relates to what and asking questions such as this one: "Do such and such procedures actually examine and deal with such and such issues that they claim to?" Are the findings or conclusions of the audit process supported by the procedures employed?

Even in the financial world, the relationship between procedures and conclusions is slippery. An accountant may find that the organization being audited meets GAAP but is not really in good overall financial shape. Accountants have weaseled by pronouncing an ongoing concern "OK" only to have it go "belly up" thereafter. The numerous stockholder lawsuits against accounting firms for their alleged "failures" to take note of the situation beyond simply meeting GAAP have been the subject of million-dollar court battles over the years. The result has been the courts ruling that, if accountants know of any condition that would jeopardize the claims of the financial proceedings, practices, or records of the concern being audited and cast doubt on the long-term credibility of an organization to survive, *they must report it in the audit.* The courts have stretched *validity* beyond simply meeting GAAP.

In auditing, consistency is a virtue for it is the key to comparison. If concern "A" is pronounced healthy, and concern "B" not healthy, one must depend upon the fact that the procedures used were the same, or no case can be made about organizational "health" and the judgments rendered in both cases are suspect. Credibility of the audit process is thus anchored to consistency of approach.

D. *The Condition of Independence*

Auditors cannot be a part of the organization they review, for it is generally conceded by the public and the press that sufficient motivation may exist to be less than rigorous, full, or candid in the disclosure of the findings. Peter Drucker (1973, p. 628), the international management guru, noted that "the governing organ of a corporation was always the last group to hear of trouble in the great business catastrophes of this century."

Why were such governing organs blind about their own troubles? The answer partly lies in the circumstance that there was insufficient protection for those persons who knew enough about such conditions to expose them. The only way an internal audit function can work is for it to be protected and shielded from influence. Even with such protections in place, an organization can fail because this function was compromised.

In a less dramatic way, even researchers have to guard against their own biases or interests taking over and clouding their judgments or conclusions. A recommendation by Lincoln and Guba (1985, p. 210) on forms of qualitative research notes:

> It is essential that adequate records (an audit trail) be kept of such action, whether in the form of file memos, minutes of longer sessions, attestations from debriefers, research syntheses and so on. Each investigator should keep a personal journal in which his or her own methodological decisions are recorded and made available for public scrutiny.

E. The Presence of Objectivity

The distinction between *objectivity* and *subjectivity* has long been a discussion point in philosophical inquiry. Can a person really be apart from that which is being observed? Every observation begins with a point of view or a person would not know what to look for or even where to start. The notion of pure inductive inquiry beginning with "unadulterated" observation has been effectively destroyed as being nonoperational in the real world (see Popper, 1959). In this sense, all observation is *biased,* if by nothing else than language and culture.

On the other hand, belief alone cannot establish something as true. For example, the widespread opinion of most scientists in the nineteenth century that female intelligence was inferior to male intelligence did not make it so (see Gould, 1981). It is possible that some statements are actually true when most people do not believe them to be so. This fact invalidates a purely subjective notion of truth.

Objectivity is therefore a *regulative notion* or *principle* (Popper, 1960/1985, p. 185) rather than an absolute standard or referent. It means that one goes about conducting an inquiry to *keep working at discovering truth* without ever believing one has necessarily found it. One is more interested in *truthfulness* than *truth*. The former is established by a continued pursuit never culminated. The latter represents an absolute condition attained. Such absolutes do not exist in the real world or in audits of organizations functioning there.

4.4 Critical Assumptions of Curriculum Audits

Assumption 1: Organizational control is a necessary part of effective design and delivery of curriculum. The curriculum audit is an application of the fiduciary audit process. As such, the process is influenced by assumptions regarding financial processes in human organizations. The most important of these assumptions relates to control.

The protection of funds in an organization requires a *control system* that safeguards them and provides for tracking their expenditure through individuals who are responsible and accountable. These persons can be brought to trial and judged if funds are misused or turn up missing. The general idea behind control in human organizations is a single line of accountability called the *chain of command* being present and a narrow division of labor or specialization being incorporated into the fiduciary function.

For example, every year, at least one story turns up about some former low-level bookkeeper running off with funds from a school district and being caught. The following investigation reveals that this person not only wrote the checks but verified the vendors who submitted purchase orders to be paid. This combination of functions may lead to the temptation to set up a dummy account in some bank that is operated by the bookkeeper, who then issues checks to the false account.

Accounting controls require that functions be divided up so that such events require collusion to pull off. The more people required to collude in fraud, the more likely it is to be detected and eventually reported and corrected.

Financial controls require specialization and separation of functions. They require some kind of superior/subordinate relationship of offices that leads to hierarchies and ultimately to bureaucracy. Financial paperwork is usually the most elaborate contrivance of most human institutions and agencies.

A question can be posed about the similarity between a curriculum in a school or school system and its financial transactions. Are they similar enough to be applicable to the same sorts of ideas about *control*? If not, then is an *audit* (in the financial sense) possible? If possible, is it desirable?

Any observer of school system operations must come away with the observation that there are many kinds of activities that, if not audits, certainly closely resemble them in appearance and application.

Among them would be federally required program audits, management reviews of various functions such as data processing or transportation, and accreditation activities. Nearly all of these involve the development of standards or conventions, examination of data and reports, interviews, observations, and the creation of recommendations to those responsible and accountable for changes and improvements. At least with accreditation, curriculum is assumed to be one of the important variables being examined, and judgments are developed about its conceptualization and development as well as various aspects of its delivery, that is, acceptance, adequacy, and results or outcomes.

Rarely, if ever, would an accreditation review recommend a level of educational reform that would resemble a revolution. Nearly all such standards involved are reflections of the status quo embodied in accepted conventions and notions. So accreditation reviews tend to reinforce prevailing organizational norms of control and ideas about accountability. For this reason, few, if any, accreditation reviews ever sparked deep educational reform.

Although curriculum audits differ from accreditation reviews in both the nature of the training required to perform them and in the standards used, they do not differ much in respect to the assumptions regarding organizational control.

Curriculum in both processes is viewed as part of, and not separate from, the control processes that may exist in the organization. Both types of reviews *assume* that someone (a person) is ultimately responsible for the scope, quality, adequacy, and utility of the curriculum.

In the current notion of accountability, the one person responsible is the *superintendent of schools.* Curriculum audits do not challenge this assertion.

For this reason, some critics of audits and accreditation may dismiss them as simple devices to perpetuate what they view as an incorrect or, worse, corrupt system of administrative controls continuing to be dominant within school systems. Some advocates of teacher "empowerment" are likely to take this view because they believe the current structure of administrative control is out of date, bankrupt, or ineffective.

Although audits can be used to review different forms of organizational control that are not "rational" or goal driven, auditing as a process does not require or force changes in the assumptions about control that any organization has decided to adopt. Rather, audits *accept them as a given* in performing such a review (English, 1988, pp. 329-342). The audit then compares the organization and its control assumptions with its own standards and objectives, unless the organization desires the auditors to question these as well. Both audits and accreditation reviews function largely within accepted notions regarding administrative-organizational controls.

Assumption 2: Curriculum is purposive, created by design, and therefore reproducible. Another critical assumption of the audit is that curriculum is a purposive creation of a school or school system. It therefore has design elements based on ideas about the kinds of purposes and functions it is to fulfill in schools. As such, it is reproducible over time. These points may appear to be obvious but they are not. There are some educators who believe that curriculum is "spontaneous," that is, a contrivance of the occasion something like the "teachable moment." Such spontaneous designs are not reproducible at all in the sense that most educators envision them. There could be nothing like a curriculum guide if curriculum itself were not more permanent. The notion of permanency, however, is based on the idea that schools have procedures, routines, and cycles of repetition and hence *stability*. Without stability in schools, current concepts of curriculum fall by the wayside. Auditing also would be of a different nature as there would be a deemphasis on document review as a source of data.

Assumption 3: There are generally accepted ideas regarding curriculum design and delivery. The curriculum field is rife with dissent about curriculum's purpose and form in schools. It is no longer considered "engineering" based on a neutral value system being dominant by which curriculum is created.

The curriculum audit uses as its substitute for GAAP generally accepted ideas about organizational functions. The literature base supporting auditing from which its standards are derived comes from two broad streams of research and opinion. They are (a) generally accepted notions about effective organizations (see Mintzberg, 1983) and (b) the effective schools and mastery learning research (see Bloom, 1981).

Actually, there is much in common in these two streams of research and opinion. At times, they are mutually reinforcing of one another. For example, both streams emphasize the development of goals and objectives, planning, discipline, and purposive behavior of leaders (see English, 1987).

The rationale for the use of this literature base for the development of audit standards is that (a) schools are organizations like many others and contain generic elements that are responsive to general ideas regarding change (see Hasenfeld, 1983) and (b) curriculum is a kind of organizational *work plan* by which the system focuses itself and delivers its primary *work tasks*. As such, it must fit the type of *work task structure* that is dominant within the organization (see Mintzberg, 1983). The result is the development of audit standards that reflect organizational design and operational contingencies that most experts in the field would agree constitute an effective organization. In this paradigm, curriculum is conceptualized as simply an educational work plan *peculiar to educational organizations* but not differing substantially in function from equivalents found in other public service agencies. Other organizations have work plans, they simply call them by different names.

The audit views curriculum as having two functions in educational systems. The first function is to *focus* the work of teachers. The second function is to *connect* the work of teachers. This view moves far beyond the idea that curriculum is a *symbolic* document for legitimizing anything teachers might choose to do in schoolrooms under generic labels or slogans.

A curriculum auditor is trained to look for any document that in real schools focuses and connects teaching. In real life, this is rarely the curriculum guide. The document that serves as the only functional tool to focus and connect the work of teachers is usually the textbook, for better or worse. Auditors differentiate between functional and symbolic documents used in schools.

If curriculum is viewed as the work plan in schools, then it encompasses virtually any document or source that in the day-to-day business of teaching focuses and connects the work of teachers. These include curriculum guides, scope and sequence charts, textbooks, state guidelines, old college notes, or anything else referenced by teachers in their work.

There always is a work plan in schools. It simply may not be the curriculum guide. The question being asked in this quest is this: "What is the *real* curriculum in the school?" Once the auditor knows the answer to this question, then a host of additional ones follow. For example, if the textbook is the real curriculum, then what are the criteria for its adoption? What is taken into account by the system officials in this process: alignment to local or state objectives, tests? (See Courts, 1991.)

From the functional perspective of what is actually going on in schools, textbook adoption is the single most important curriculum decision made by school officials and boards of education because that decision significantly affects what teachers do when the classroom door is shut.

Curriculum academics make a significant mistake by viewing curriculum development and textbook adoption as separate processes. This split leads to the continued domination of textbooks in schools to direct the work of teachers and to the fact that textbooks substitute for curriculum itself. This happens even when schools have created curriculum guides that are supposed to "direct" teachers in the use of textbooks.

The concept of curriculum as work plans refocuses the attention away from symbolic documents and toward ones that are functional and, incidentally, when pursued as a design for curriculum development, help the textbook become the means to the end instead of being a substitute for the end (i.e., it becomes a validated local curriculum).

When teaching as an activity in schools is guided, configured, shaped, and directed by *curriculum* (as the work plan), then *instruction* is the result. A curriculum auditor looks at instruction as the act of teaching influenced by curriculum. This view captures the obvious fact that teaching is going on in schools even when there is no curriculum (guide). There is usually a work plan of some kind involved, however. When the work plan is used by teachers to shape and direct their work, the product is instruction. Auditors look for instruction and the documents employed by a school system to shape it.

This has become more critical than ever because virtually all tests assume that instruction is present in some form. Tests that assess the impact of cumulative learning assume there has been cumulative teaching. Teaching alone will not improve test scores. Teaching has to be *aligned* (on task) and purposive (cumulative).

It was this cumulative notion that Ralph Tyler addressed in his famous question in 1949 (p. 83), "How can learning experiences be organized for effective instruction?" No matter how inspirational and motivational teaching per se may be, if unfocused and unconnected, improved assessment scores do not occur until these flaws are removed by the presence of functional, aligned curriculum. No curriculum auditor ever assumes that unfocused and unconnected teaching, no matter how inspirational, will ever be enough to create a school system from a system of schools.

Assumption 4: The unit of analysis is the school or the school system. The curriculum audit assumes that the focus of the audit, the basic *unit of analysis,* is the school or the school system.

The continuing movement toward a national curriculum and a national exam will focus even harder on school systems simply because tests assess cumulative things and not knowledge or skills learned only at one school with any curricular or learning continua.

To improve test or assessment performance, more than one grade level is involved. This condition shifts the emphasis on the improvement of performance to multiple years and reinforces the need for a sound curriculum that is sequenced properly to enable the tested knowledge to be taught or retaught if necessary.

The improvement of test performance always involves strengthening the interconnectedness of curriculum across grade levels and ultimately across schools. This phenomenon is a decidedly *centralizing tendency* rather than a decentralizing one. The current move toward site-based management acts to decrease pupil responses on many standardized and criterion-referenced tests because it raises the distinct probability that the interconnectedness of the curriculum will be jeopardized.

The more options schools pursue, the more likely it will be that they select different curricula than that being tested or pursue it in different sequential relationships that result in curriculum skew and test skew being at opposite ends. One result is that, while the curriculum may be more interesting to both teachers and students, test scores decline. This scenario has a name and it is *suboptimization.* Suboptimization refers to the fact that, within some systems, subparts are successful while the larger system fails, or the subsystem succeeds at the *expense of the larger system.*

A curriculum auditor focuses on the unit of analysis and what it will take to enable it to be successful within the *conditions and goals/objectives it has selected for itself.* If the system has selected a strategy of decentralization, then the auditor will accept this as a given and look for evidence that contradicts the selection, pointing out that it may not be successful unless conditions are rectified and changed to become harmonious.

For example, if the system indicates it wants to site base all curriculum decisions to the school level, then the system should also site base its evaluation strategies as well. That would be congruent. If the system site bases curriculum decision making to the school level but retains testing, however, then the auditor will point out the obvious contradiction that is occurring. In this case, the system is working at opposite purposes. Something will have to give. Either the system will abandon centralized testing, or the schools will surrender at least that portion of the curriculum that is tested centrally to central dictates. All of this kind of debate occurs in the initial selection of the unit of audit analysis.

Assumption 5: School systems are rational entities. A *rational* system is one in which the people and the activities are directed by goals and objectives (Silver, 1983, p. 77). Most practitioners assume that organizational life in school systems is quite rational. The natural activities that flow from such a decision are planning, budgeting, scheduling, curriculum development, testing, promotion, grouping, grading, and teaching.

There are, at least theoretically, certain questions about whether system rationality really exists. In fact, there is some evidence and thought that educators make decisions and then create plans that follow, making it appear that rationality is present when it is not (Weick, 1985).

If school systems are not rational, however, they have to *pretend to be* to survive in a world that believes they should be and forces them to compete for funds to continue operating on this basis. There are few circumstances in the real world where state legislators or boards of education will be very responsive to a statement such as this one: "We don't really know where we are going, but trust us to get there." That confession would be unthinkable even if it were true.

So curriculum audits operate on the premise that there is system rationality present and that it is possible to improve the relationship between internal activities and external performance, however measured.

4.5 Curriculum Audit Standards

Curriculum audits employ five standards. All of them are related to assumptions regarding organizational effectiveness, in which curriculum is viewed as a *facilitating function* by which its performance can be improved over time. Curriculum is therefore a means to an end and *not* an end in itself. A successful or "good" curriculum is one that enables the system to *attain its objectives*. These are viewed as compatible and in some cases congruent with objectives designed for students. Most of the time, they are perceived as one and the same.

Curriculum audit standards emanate from an idea called *quality control* (English, 1978). Quality control is a nearly universal concept with many applications to industry, government, and public service organizations, including education (Juran, 1979).

At the heart of the curriculum audit is the idea that quality control should be functional in a school system. That means that there are clear goals or objectives; human activity is directed toward accomplishing them; feedback is gathered about system performance (internal and external); and such data are used to examine current levels of performance in order to change things to subsequently improve performance. When this concept is iteratively employed over time, there should be a systematic overall improvement of performance. If that level of performance becomes dramatically better, and is sustained over time, it is called a *breakthrough*. Now more than ever, American education is being called upon to engage in a breakthrough of truly national proportions as embodied in the Bush "America 2000" initiative.

The three elements of quality control are present in the form of (a) written curriculum in some form being present, which is related to (or aligned with) the (b) tested curriculum, which (c) becomes the taught curriculum as designed. In this situation, both curriculum design and delivery are connected to maximize pupil performance.

In real life, there are many ways a school system can create and maintain quality control. The system could begin by going down the road of improving teaching, that is, *delivery.* The system will soon discover, however, that, if all it is doing is delivering an unconnected curriculum better, pupil performance (at least on tests) does not necessarily improve (English & Steffy, 1983).

The problem is not delivery but *design,* that is, an unaligned and unconnected curriculum that is being taught better. Poor curriculum taught better is not an improvement but oddly a detriment to improved test performance. When the system and its officials make adjustments to a strategy aimed at improving delivery, but that now includes attention to design (including alignment), it has adopted the notion of quality control. The standards of the audit embody the concept of quality control.

Standard 1: The school district is able to demonstrate its control of resources, programs, and personnel. The issue of control is faced squarely in the first standard of the audit. The audit asserts that control is exhibited politically in acts of the elected or appointed board of education functioning within a quasi-state system of schools. Therefore it has an obligation to become congruent with that system. It has a legal mandate to carry out the larger system's purpose and objectives, and it must employ legal and organizational/structural means to do so. An auditor examines these relationships to determine whether there are inconsistencies or contradictions.

A *finding* in an audit is a statement of discrepancy between a standard and a validated (called "triangulated") condition ascertained by the auditors. In this case, the auditor may find that "the Board of Education of Valley Stream School District is not evaluating personnel in keeping with the provisions of [state law, federal regulation]" or the like. This calls attention to a *discrepancy* regarding control to which the educational entity being audited must adhere.

The areas where auditors look for evidence of control are planning and policy development. The existence of plans, whether they are long, short, or strategic, and a policy framework are considered strong evidence that a school system is in control of itself. Of course, there are two aspects of control: *design* (the plans and the policies) and *delivery* (assessing their impact on operations).

Auditors examine the quality of plans and policies based on a number of criteria. Among them are clarity, inclusiveness, and recency. Plans and policies should be unambiguous, contain all of the elements of quality control, and be periodically updated.

The auditor assumes that it is the elected or appointed board of education that is responsible for the creation and mainte-nance of policies and plans. Among the responsibilities for poli-cies and plans are their implementation, monitoring, and altering/updating when required. The curriculum audit as-sumes that a board of education is active rather than passive and has not been captured by a superintendent who has as-sumed these functions. The board of education has a definite role in the curriculum design and delivery process, which in-cludes the evaluation of the entire process including the super-intendency.

Standard 2: The school district has established clear and valid objectives for students. In this audit standard, the auditors are looking for the presence of instructional objectives to guide classroom teachers in the delivery of the curriculum (see Dick & Carey, 1978).

Most of the time, such objectives are found in either (a) cur-riculum guides or (b) textbooks. All curriculum guides in the school district are rated by the auditors on an instrument that examines (a) the clarity of objectives, (b) the congruence of the objectives to the testing program (curriculum alignment), (c) the scope and sequence of the curriculum at levels below and above the designated one being examined, (d) the delineation by objec-tive of the major instructional tools to be used in the delivery of the curriculum, and (e) the presence of "cues" by which the teacher can move easily from the curriculum to the construction of the appropriate learning environment in the classroom.

All curriculum guides that teachers may use in classrooms in the entire school district are rated and ranked. These data pro-vide the system with an idea of the strengths and weaknesses of the curriculum, its patterns, and its design flaws as well as the extent to which it is being used in classrooms. The latter finding comes not from rating curriculum guides but from interviews of classroom teachers.

The "quality" of a curriculum within the parameters of a curriculum audit is simply its ability to designate the key points of quality control for application in the classroom. The teacher is the one who exercises quality control, and so the documents from which the teacher would manage it must contain all of the aspects of it.

Thus the curriculum guide is considered a "stand-alone" document; that is, no other document is necessary to provide the directions for quality control in the classroom. There is then a tight linkage between guides, textbooks, tests, and significant cues for teachers to clearly translate these relationships into practice.

Standard 3: The school district is able to direct its resources consistently and equitably to accomplish its mission. This standard of the curriculum audit is often called the "equity standard" because, via documents, auditors look for a planned consistency through goals and objectives, plans and policies, and the way resources such as instructional time, dollar allocation, books, technology, and the like are distributed throughout the schools.

It is at this stage that auditors examine the effects of tracking and whether this practice has resulted in inequities such as resegregation by race of students in the bottom tracks or whether access to certain programs is equitable for all students.

One of the most penetrating types of analyses occurs when auditors search for predictable and predictive linkages from board policies or program content objectives to classroom objectives. That is, can classroom objectives and their configuration from program objectives be predicted from one level to the other? If any given configuration of one level of objectives to the next is not anticipated or described, then the auditors may conclude that nearly any configuration will do and the school system is not in control of the internal processes of translation from one level of the organization to the next.

For example, one level of the organization occurs at the program's focus, that is, K-12 science, social studies, math, and so on. The next level might be at a grade level in the elementary school or the course level at the secondary school. By analyzing and classifying objectives at the course level across to the program level, the auditor establishes a configuration (or distribution) of "matches" from one to the other. One might say, then, that 89% of the course objectives in social studies are clustered around one districtwide social studies goal or objective. Then, if that districtwide goal were taught, it would account for 89% of all the objectives for that course.

For an auditor to accept this relationship as evidence of "consistency," this distribution has to be predicted or described somewhere in the system as "proper" or "adequate." If such a statement is found, then the distribution of objectives at one level was predicted or anticipated by the other. Under this scenario, the district is said to exercise "control."

Most curricula in school systems are not consistent because curriculum at the classroom level is developed in isolation from district-level objectives or goals, or such district-level goals are so nebulous as to be incapable of providing much direction to development at lower levels except in a symbolic sense.

Unless lower-level objectives are predicted by upper levels, however, there can be no "control" from one level to the next. The fact that such breakdowns are rather common is what led Weick (1978) to label educational systems as "loosely coupled." The curriculum auditor does not accept this as a desirable state of affairs. A school system cannot be accountable unless it is in control of itself as well as its own internal operations.

Standard 4: The school district uses the results from district-designed and/or adopted instruments to adjust, improve, or terminate ineffective practices or programs. This standard of the audit is concerned with the use of feedback and its applications and connections internally to improve operations within a school system.

To be useful, data must be able to be connected to the goals and objectives of whatever unit is expected to apply them to their functions. For example, if the graduation rate is influenced by a test score on a statewide exam, the passing and failing rates must be able to be connected to the places in the school system that have the most to do with them.

An item analysis of the exam scores that showed which areas were not learned should be traceable back to segments of the curriculum and should be retaught. This connection, or the ability to make it, is the essence of *feedback*.

The use of feedback has two parts. The first is the disaggregation of the data from the test. The second is the reconnection of the disaggregated data to the curriculum in some form. When the data are reconnected, the work plan is changed so that, with reteaching, more students pass the exam with subsequent teaching and testing.

Feedback comes in a variety of forms in addition to test scores. It comes in the form of college acceptance rates, graduate follow-up studies regarding what students perceived the strengths and weaknesses to be in the curriculum, or community surveys and opinions about the schools.

Too often, curriculum auditors find that school districts are "data rich" but "information poor." Most school systems have more data than they know how to use. Data become information when their utility has been established and someone finds them functional in terms of being able to engage in decision making based upon them.

Auditors examine school systems for any kind of data that the district possesses that it may use to make decisions about the design and the delivery of the curriculum. Data sources are examined for trends. Trends are shown longitudinally. Are scores going up or down? Are there changes within the scores and, if so, what are they? Have school district officials charted these trends? Are they aware of them? How are data reported to the board and the public? (See Lyman, 1971.)

Auditors also examine the extent to which data provide relevant information about all the curriculum, not just the basic skills or a narrow definition of "academics." If a school system is using a statewide test of some sort for assessing the rudiments of computing, reading, and writing, how are other areas of the curriculum assessed, if at all? How are music, art, social studies, science, and the like assessed on a comparable basis? If they are not assessed, why not?

A curriculum auditor wants to know not only what is assessed in the curriculum but what is not assessed as well as the possible reasons for the nonassessment. Auditors are also prepared to deal with the data that are not derived from standardized tests or other kinds of bench marks that are school system quality indicators.

Standard 5: The school district has improved productivity. The last standard is often called "the *so what* standard." It is one that deals with the *meaning* of quality control. If a school system has developed valid objectives, created curricular work plans that include and link them to the schools, and teachers use them, and if resources are allocated equitably and consistently, and if results of these applications are systematically assessed and the data disaggregated and reapplied to curricular adjustments over time, so what? Are children learning more? Are they learning better? Are schools better and more humane places? (See Tuckman, 1985.)

The audit could assess productivity if the school district had the data base by which the assessment could be conducted. Productivity in simplistic form is merely a determination of whether outputs are up, given a decrease in inputs or at least the same level of inputs being continued. That means that results (however defined or measured) have improved as costs have remained steady or decreased (see Walberg, 1979).

Such determinations in school systems present innumerable difficulties, among them the fact that, as a labor-intensive human organization, "people costs" account for nearly 70%-80% of the budget, and it is difficult to "control" them or find ways to trade off cost increases with subsequent "savings" elsewhere such as the installation of technology and the like commonly found in manufacturing examples of productivity computation. For this and other reasons, manufacturing models are not completely suitable for the computation of productivity in schools (see Posavac & Carey, 1989).

Auditors therefore do not expect to find absolute measures for productivity in schools. They do expect to find *relative* measures, and they do expect to find some basic indicators that the system has linked its budgetary projections to outcomes. This "bridge" between cost projections and expected results requires some kind of programmed budget. The programmed budget acts as a tool to link costs to results or *benefits* as they are sometimes called (see Hartman, 1988, p. 27).

Traditional "line item" budgeting cannot be used to link costs to benefits or results. Without alterations in the ways school budgets are conceptualized and implemented in most school systems, the determination of productivity is nearly impossible to assess, except perhaps as with very gross models using inputs compared with results on standardized tests (see Murnane, 1975). Such determinations are so crude, and the tests such unreliable indicators of local school district curricular objectives, that whatever cost/benefits are discerned are nearly useless in the day-to-day operations of most school districts for determining productivity and improving it with rational actions.

These are the five basic standards of the curriculum audit. Taken collectively, they constitute a powerful way to assess the quality of school district curriculum management that is present in school systems.

4.6 Anticipating the Results
of a Curriculum Audit

What kinds of results could school system officials expect if they underwent a curriculum audit? Are there patterns in what auditors commonly find? The only data base that exists to answer this question has been in Kentucky, where nearly 10% of the school systems (of 177 districts) have been audited within the last three years.

Steffy (1989-1990) reviewed the findings of five audits conducted in Kentucky and examined the results to ascertain common findings. She categorized the systems audited by separating them into two categories: those requiring state intervention (called Phase III districts) and those not requiring state intervention (called Phase I districts). Audits were therefore conducted in "good" districts (Phase I) and "poor" ones (Phase III) according to state standards.

Findings that separated these two types of school systems were that, in Phase I districts, there was substantially better control exhibited in the curriculum audit data than in Phase III districts. She noted that, while none of the five school systems had a strategic or long-range plan, the Phase I districts had "informal long-range planning" that was not present in the Phase III districts at all. Phase I districts also showed evidence of board and superintendent priorities being present that were absent in the Phase III systems.

One of the biggest differences between the systems monitored was that Phase I districts all had designed and employed staff training for various curriculum problems. None of the Phase III systems had implemented this procedure.

An area where both types of districts were deficient occurred with Standard 4, the use of feedback. "None of districts audited appeared to have a formalized process in place to terminate ineffective programs based on program effectiveness data" (Steffy, 1989-1990, p. 14). Budgeting practices in the Phase III districts clearly separated curriculum and finance; that is, there was no relationship between these two types of activities. In Phase I districts, there was strong evidence of informal linkages between these two processes.

These data suggest that poor test scores, lack of control over finances, deficient board policies, lack of staff development, and lack of adequate planning evidenced in the curriculum audit do earmark school systems having problems in being responsive to state mandates designed to improve operations and student achievement. At least in Kentucky, however, such mandates are still not rigorous enough to require even "good" school systems to do better because of the lack of formalized procedures to link actions to results. Curriculum audits can therefore improve operations in both "good" and "poor" school systems.

4.7 The Difference Between Auditing and Accreditation

Although curriculum audits and regional accreditation often involve examining schools for the same bench marks (such as the presence of plans, objectives, curriculum, tests, and the like), they differ in several fundamental respects.

Audits compare triangulated results with standards and simply report them. Accreditation reports sometimes do the same thing but then have to use the data to make a decision: to accredit or not. Accreditation agencies then have to determine how many areas can be deficient and still enable a school to "pass" the accreditation process. This necessity tends to "flatten out" the individual findings of an accreditation report and focus on the outcome.

Audits do not have any process to arrive at a summative judgment. Findings are reported individually by standard. All of them are important. Each is addressed in the audit's recommendations.

Audits rarely offer "commendations." Rather, school systems are expected to possess the characteristics being examined. If they have them, they are not commended for what should be "standard operating procedure." In the words of one auditor, the railroad doesn't get commended if the trains run on time. They are supposed to be on time.

The second major difference between auditors and those serving on accreditation teams is that audit training is much more rigorous. To become an auditor, one must be invited at the conclusion of a five and a half day training program to enter an internship. The five and a half day program consists of learning how to write in the audit style, with major writing assignments that are reviewed by several trained auditors and returned with feedback and recommendations for improvement.

An audit internship is a situation where the prospective auditor engages in an actual audit and writes a piece of it under the supervision of a trained auditor. This too must be successfully accomplished before a person can become an auditor.

Accreditation training is far less rigorous and the standards for writing are not as high. Any examination of a typical accreditation report will reveal major differences in style, content, focus, and clarity within the respective sections of the final report. Accreditation reports are often very uneven in all of these areas. Audits are much more focused and consistent in this regard.

The composition of the actual audit versus accreditation teams is another factor. In Kentucky, for example, audit teams are staffed half by insiders to the state and half by outsiders, with the lead auditor always being from out of state. This selection and staffing process ensures objectivity and balance and lessens the probability that political pressure or colleague influence will "soften" the final report. Accreditation, as a process, is too open to "back scratching" to have the confidence of the public that the system or the school was really rigorously examined and with findings publicly reported. In the words of a seasoned lead auditor, "The worst schools I've ever audited were all accredited."

Accreditation is cheaper than auditing. While auditors are individually paid a fee and expenses, accreditation team members usually only have their expenses reimbursed. This keeps the costs down for the school being examined but results in a less than demanding scenario for a quality report.

Accreditation agencies must somehow keep enough of their members happy enough to continue to operate. Therefore their standards are less rigorous and the final determination on a school to be accredited does permit noncompliance with some areas being examined. Curriculum audits do not have to confront these problems. Audit standards are not compromised by the same requirements. Accreditation as a process remains valuable, often more for the members doing the accrediting than for the school being examined, but it cannot be considered a "safety net" for eliminating poor practices in the schools except in the most blatant cases.

4.8 After a Curriculum Audit, Then What?

The curriculum audit provides a superintendent and a board with tremendous political leverage to engage in larger change at a faster pace than if one had not been completed. The data base of the audit and its immediacy in a public report create the *expectancy* of a response that is comprehensive. In part, the response is shaped by the audit's recommendations, which are geared to meet all of the findings reported.

Because the audit is a comprehensive, though select, examination, and because it has thoroughly examined all of the relevant documents, interviewed the key persons from top to bottom in the system, and visited nearly all of the schools, the "data sweep" inclusiveness is a formidable one upon which to recommend changes. On these grounds alone, few will be able to argue against the content of change. So any dispute must occur over the time table for the changes rather than the nature of the changes proposed per se.

The potency of the audit lies in its public nature. The more public it is, the greater the leverage for change. The best approach is to reveal the audit completely, make copies available for everyone who wants to read it by including copies in the public libraries, and build the consensual base for actions on the findings. A school system cannot afford to be defensive about the findings. In the words of one seasoned superintendent, "We didn't bring these people 2,000 miles to pat us on the back. We wanted the most demanding examination we could find and we got it. Now, here is what we are going to do about it." That posture simply eliminates the inevitable tendency of some of the public to want to find a scapegoat(s) for the deficiencies reported in the audit.

As the audit is released, it is often accompanied by a draft "action plan" and response by the superintendent to each finding. That shows the public what the school system officials are going to do about each finding and recommendation.

Auditors are careful to point out that the board of education never "adopts" an audit, it "receives" an audit. Audits are never accepted until the superintendent has had an opportunity to respond, to agree or disagree with the findings and the recommendations proposed. The audit process is therefore one to ensure that accountability remains within the chain of command of the school district.

4.9 Is Your School or District Ready for a Curriculum Audit?

To assist the reader in determining whether his or her school or school district is ready for a curriculum audit, the following checklist has been developed. Of course, an audit can be completed even if a school or school district is "not ready," and it can be used to speed up "readiness." Most school system officials, however, desire an audit to reveal what additional steps ought to be taken to complete a good curriculum management system already being put into operation. The audit itself then is a kind of evaluation of how well the district has progressed in developing local control of its own curriculum. The checklist is not centered on the audit standards but does include them.

Checklist to Determine Readiness for a Curriculum Audit

Area to Be Examined	*Conditions That Pertain*

Board Policies

1. Is there a comprehensive set of board policies that establish the framework for curriculum quality control (written, taught, and tested)? _____
2. Do the policies contain statements regarding alignment, testing, and textbook adoption? _____
3. Is there a policy that links budget development to curriculum development so that curriculum leads as opposed to follows the budget? _____
4. Do policies clearly establish the responsibilities for curriculum design and delivery in the system? _____

5. Do policies establish the means to ensure equitability of resource flow and consistency of that flow across all schools in the system?   _____

6. Do policies specify the nature of public reports in all areas of quality control and indicate the board's role in monitoring them?   _____

School Administrators and Supervisors

1. Do administrators and supervisors understand curricular quality control and the implications for their respective responsibilities in terms of carrying it out?   _____

2. Has any confusion between line and staff been eliminated in the design and delivery of curriculum?   _____

3. Do principals know how to monitor the delivery of curriculum in their schools?   _____

4. Do principals know how to disaggregate test data and work with teachers in reconnecting it to the curriculum?   _____

5. Do teachers know how to apply and modify the curriculum to obtain better results in their classrooms?   _____

The Curriculum

1. Is curriculum in the district functional? Does it enable the system to focus and connect the work of teachers, to tighten or loosen, as necessary?   _____

2. Is curriculum aligned with the existing tests to obtain maximum congruence? _____

3. Is curriculum aligned with the major textbooks to ensure that curriculum leads rather than follows textbook adoption? _____

4. Does functional curriculum exist for all areas taught in the school system? _____

5. Are teachers following the curriculum? _____

6. Has the district taken steps to validate its curriculum as the most appropriate of those it could be using? _____

7. Has the district taken steps to ensure that the curriculum can be taught within the time available? _____

8. Is there enough flexibility within the curriculum to adapt it to various learner differences that exist in the system? _____

9. Does the curriculum provide for continuity and consistency in the instructional program? _____

Tests and Assessment

1. Are tests selected because of their match to local curriculum? _____

2. Are areas of the curriculum that are not formally assessed evaluated with some other appropriate means? _____

3. Are test data regularly disaggregated and linked back to the curriculum to ensure enhanced pupil performance on subsequent test administrations? _____

4. Is the public systematically informed about test results and strengths and weaknesses of tests?   _____

5. Do teachers make systematic use of test data to alter their work?   _____

6. Do tests measure more than the lower levels of cognition and attitude development?   _____

7. Are test data used to categorize students unfairly by race or sex or to relegate groups of students to a system of grouping that discourages them from learning?   _____

Budget Development

1. Does the budget follow or precede curricular priorities?   _____

2. Does the budget fully support curricular priorities?   _____

3. Is there sufficient detail in the budget to link it to programs and to costs?   _____

4. Does the budget provide for a means to evaluate the wisdom of dollar allocations to specific fiscal/curricular targets?   _____

5. Are fiscal priorities linked to a formal planning process in the district?   _____

6. Can fiscal requests be shaped by school and program priorities outside of the formulas used?   _____

Productivity

1. Do district officials know that dollars spent have resulted in improved pupil learning?   _____

2. Do district officials know
   whether the dollars spent in
   terms of planning priorities
   have resulted in obtaining the
   desired results?   _____
3. Has the district been able to
   improve its operations without
   necessarily spending any
   additional dollars?   _____
4. Have programs that have not
   improved over time been
   changed or terminated?   _____

A large number of affirmative answers to these questions, with subsequent details as to how and under what conditions they are and continue to be affirmative, may indicate that the school or school district is ready to have a curriculum audit. Negative answers indicate any areas where there are discrepancies between operations and audit standards.

Of course, the application of these questions to existing school district operations could be pursued as a matter of internal auditing as well, as long as the drawbacks to doing audits internally are considered as compared with those of external auditing.

The curriculum audit has emerged in the decade of the 1980s as a powerful way of examining curricular quality control in schools. All of the evidence indicates that it will grow in use and application in the new millennium.

References

Bloom, B. S. (1981). *All our children learning.* New York: McGraw-Hill.
Courts, P. L. (1991). *Literacy and empowerment.* South Hadley, MA: Bergin & Garvey.
Dick, W., & Carey, L. (1978). *The systematic design of instruction.* Glenview, IL: Scott, Foresman.
Drucker, P. F. (1973). *Management.* New York: Harper & Row.
Elashoff, J. D., & Snow, R. E. (1971). *Pygmalion reconsidered.* Belmont, CA: Wadsworth.
English, F. W. (1978). *Quality control in curriculum development.* Arlington, VA: American Association of School Administrators.

English, F. W. (1987). *Curriculum management for schools, colleges, business.* Springfield, IL: Charles C Thomas.

English, F. W. (1988). *Curriculum auditing.* Lancaster, PA: Technomic.

English, F. W., & Steffy, B. E. (1983, February). Differentiating between design and delivery problems in achieving quality control in school curriculum management. *Educational Technology, 13,* 29-32.

Gould, S. J. (1981). *The mismeasure of man.* New York: Norton.

Hartman, W. T. (1988). *School district budgeting.* Englewood Cliffs, NJ: Prentice-Hall.

Hasenfeld, Y. (1983). *Human service organizations.* Englewood Cliffs, NJ: Prentice-Hall.

Juran, J. M. (1979). *Quality control handbook.* New York: McGraw-Hill.

Lessinger, L. (1970). *Every kid a winner.* New York: Simon & Schuster.

Lincoln, Y. S., & Guba, E. G. (1985). *Naturalistic inquiry.* Beverly Hills, CA: Sage.

Lyman, H. B. (1971). *Test scores and what they mean.* Englewood Cliffs, NJ: Prentice-Hall.

Mansfield, H. C., Jr. (1989). *Taming the prince.* New York: Free Press.

Mintzberg, H. (1983). *Structure in fives: Designing effective organizations.* Englewood Cliffs, NJ: Prentice-Hall.

Murnane, R. J. (1975). *The impact of school resources on the learning of inner city children.* Cambridge, MA: Ballinger.

Popper, K. R. (1959). *The logic of scientific discovery.* New York: Harper & Row.

Popper, K. R. (1985). Truth and approximation to truth. In D. Miller (Ed.), *Popper selections.* Princeton, NJ: Princeton University Press. (Original work published 1960)

Posavac, E. J., & Carey, R. G. (1989). *Program evaluation.* Englewood Cliffs, NJ: Prentice-Hall.

Sayle, A. J. (1981). *Management audits.* London: McGraw-Hill.

Silver, P. (1983). *Educational administration: Theoretical perspectives on practice and research.* New York: Harper & Row.

Steffy, B. (1989-1990). Curriculum auditing as a state agency tool in takeovers. *National Forum of Applied Educational Research Journal, 3*(1), 5-16.

Tuckman, B. W. (1985). *Evaluating instructional programs.* Boston: Allyn & Bacon.

Tyler, R. W. (1949). *Basic principles of curriculum and instruction.* Chicago: University of Chicago Press.

Walberg, H. J. (1979). *Educational environment and effects.* Berkeley, CA: McCutchan.

Weick, K. (1978, December). Educational organizations as loosely coupled systems. *Administrative Science Quarterly, 23,* 541-552.

Weick, K. (1985). Sources of order in underorganized systems: Themes in recent organizational theory. In Y. S. Lincoln (Ed.), *Organizational theory and inquiry.* Beverly Hills, CA: Sage.

Troubleshooting Guide

Further Resources for the
Millennium Edition

Aguilera, R., & Hendricks, J. (1996). Increasing standardized achievement scores in a high risk school district. *NASSP Journal Curriculum Report, 26*(September), 1-5.

A measurement of what? (1997, September). *Black Issues in Higher Education,* pp. 18-23.

Brendt, B., & DiObilda, N. (1993). Effects of curriculum alignment versus direct instruction on urban children. *Journal of Educational Research, 86*(6), 333-338.

Chandler, D., & Brosnan, P. (1995). A comparison between mathematics textbook content and a statewide mathematics proficiency test. *School Science and Mathematics, 95*(3), 118-123.

Damelio, R. (1990). *An analysis of SB 813 school legislation's impact on curriculum alignment and student assessment efforts as perceived by district curriculum administrators.* Unpublished doctoral dissertation, University of San Francisco.

English, F. (1995). Developing, aligning, and auditing the curriculum. *The LPD Video Journal of Education, 5*(1).

English, F., & Larson, F. (1996). *Curriculum management for educational and social service organizations.* Springfield, IL: Charles C Thomas.

130 DECIDING WHAT TO TEACH AND TEST

Ferguson, L. (1994). *The art and science of holistic alignments*. Scottsdale, AZ: Evans-Newton.

Flanders, J. (1994). Textbooks, teachers, and the SIMS test. *Journal for Research in Mathematics Education, 25*(3), 260-278.

Frase, L., English, F., & Poston, W. Jr. (1995). *The curriculum management audit*. Lancaster, PA: Technomic.

Haggard, D. (1986). Curriculum alignment in North Carolina: Relationships of state mandated tests, textbooks, and objectives. *Dissertation Abstracts International, 47*(05) 1590. (University Microfilms No. AAC86-18484)

Hoyle, J., English, F., & Steffy, B. (1998). *Skills for successful 21st century school leaders*. Arlington, VA: American Association of School Administrators.

Irving, J. (1990). *Black students and school failure*. New York: Praeger.

Leitzel, T. (1993). *Platform utility/alignment between course planning and testing decisions on criterion-referenced situations*. Unpublished doctoral dissertation, Virginia Polytechnic Institute and State University.

Lynch, K. (1990). *An evaluation of curriculum alignment as a process of improving academic achievement (effective schools)*. Unpublished doctoral dissertation, University of LaVerne.

Mehler, B. (1999, Winter). Race and "reason": Academic ideas a pillar of racist thought. *Intelligence Report*, pp. 27-37.

Mitchell, F. (1998). *The effects of curriculum alignment on the mathematics achievement of third-grade students as measured by the Iowa Tests of Basic Skills: Implications for educational administrators*. Unpublished doctoral dissertation, Clark Atlanta University.

Murphy, J. (1992). *The effects of curriculum alignment on CAP scores in grades six and eight*. Unpublished doctoral dissertation, The University of LaVerne.

Price-Baugh, R. (1997). *Correlation of textbook alignment with student achievement scores*. Unpublished doctoral dissertation, Baylor University.

Reisberg, L. (1998, September). Disparities grow in SAT scores of ethnic and racial groups. *The Chronicle of Higher Education*, p. A42.

Robinson, G., & Brandon, D. (1994). *NAEP test scores: Should they be used to compare and rank state educational quality?* Arlington, VA: Educational Research Service.

Sacks, P. (1997). Standardized testing: Meritocracy's crooked yardstick. *Change, 29*(2), 24-31.

Steffy, B. (1995). *Authentic assessment and curriculum alignment: Meeting the challenge of national standards*. Rockport, MA: ProActive.

Tashakkori, A., & Teddlie, C. (1998). *Mixed methodology: Combining qualitative and quantitative approaches*. Thousand Oaks, CA: Sage.

Viadero, D. (1997, April). Surprise! Analysis links curriculum, TIMSS test scores. *Education Week*, p. 2.

Westbury, I. (1992, June/July). Comparing American and Japanese achievement: Is the U.S. really a low achiever? *Educational Researcher*, pp. 18-24.

Winfield, L., & Woodard, M. (1994). Assessment, equity, and diversity in reforming America's schools. *Educational Policy, 8*(1), 3-27.

Zellmer, M. (1997). *Effect on reading test scores when teachers are provided information that relates local curriculum documents to the test*. Unpublished doctoral dissertation, Marquette University.

CORWIN
PRESS

The Corwin Press logo—a raven striding across an open book—
represents the happy union of courage and learning. We are a
professional-level publisher of books and journals for K–12 educators, and we are committed to creating and providing resources that
embody these qualities. Corwin's motto is "Success for All Learners."